Y0-BVQ-481

URBANIZATION OF RURAL AMERICA

URBANIZATION OF RURAL AMERICA

Donald A. Henderson

HT
167
.H46
1997
West

NOVA SCIENCE PUBLISHERS, INC.
Commack, NY

Editorial Production: Susan Boriotti
Assistant Vice President/Art Director: Maria Ester Hawrys
Office Manager: Annette Hellinger
Graphics: Frank Grucci
Acquisitions Editor: Tatiana Shohov
Book Production: Ludmila Kwartiroff, Christine Mathosian,
                    Joanne Metal and Tammy Sauter
Circulation: Iyatunde Abdullah, Cathy DeGregory, and Maryanne Schmidt

Library of Congress Cataloging-in-Publication Data
available upon request

ISBN 1-56072-525-7

Copyright © 1997 by Nova Science Publishers, Inc.
            6080 Jericho Turnpike, Suite 207
            Commack, New York 11725
            Tele. 516-499-3103   Fax 516-499-3146
            E-Mail: Novascience@earthlink.net
            Web Site: http://www.nexusworld.com/nova

All rights reserved. No part of this book may be reproduced, stored in a retrieval system or transmitted in any form or by any means: electronic, electrostatic, magnetic, tape, mechanical, photocopying, recording or otherwise without permission from the publishers.

The authors and publisher haven taken care in preparation of this book, but make no expressed or implied warranty of any kind and assume no responsibility for any errors or omissions. No liability is assumed for incidental or consequential damages in connection with or arising out of information contained in this book.

This publication is designed to provide accurate and authoritative information with regard to the subject matter covered herein. It is sold with the clear understanding that the publisher is not engaged in rendering legal or any other professional services. If legal or any other expert assistance is required, the services of a competent person should be sought. FROM A DECLARATION OF PARTICIPANTS JOINTLY ADOPTED BY A COMMITTEE OF THE AMERICAN BAR ASSOCIATION AND A COMMITTEE OF PUBLISHERS.

Printed in the United States of America

CONTENTS

PART III   URBAN CENTERS FOR THE 21ST CENTURY

INTRODUCTION

Mention "Rural America" to most people and they immediately conjure up bucolic scenes of agricultural farm lands or national forest with scenic campgrounds and beautiful resorts. A great deal of these images are rapidly becoming history with nostalgic memories of what used to be in late nineteenth and early twentieth century America. Essentially two things have happened. The small American farm, as we have known it, is rapidly disappearing, and new urban communities are taking their place.

Correspondingly, if you mention "Urban America" to most people, the image of New York City, the Chicago skyline and the Los Angeles freeways along with the specter of urban decay in such places as Detroit, Washington D.C., Boston and Miami, comes to mind. Traffic congestion, oppressive population densities, public housing and an over supply of obsolete factories, retail stores and office buildings are the hallmarks of these older American cities.

If we know and understand our history, we may not have to relive it. As a bonus for such insight, we may be able to avoid repeating our past mistakes and plan intelligently for the future. If we want to understand how rural America is being urbanized and will be transformed into the cities of tomorrow and the 21st century, we must look closely at what gave rise to and produced the cities of the past. At the same time we should also examine what caused the demise of so many of these cities that are no longer with us. Human history has been a continuous struggle for survival and the advancement of mankind's comfort and contentment. Plato felt that the only way man could elevate his spirit was to eschew all mechanical and physical things and contemplate the proper philosophy for the good of man and his spirit. Cicero expressed the idea that the essence of a true gentleman was his refusal to have anything to do with things of practical utility. As we now know such a point of view was the antithesis of practically all of the improvements that have shaped our lives and created the world we live in today. And most importantly, these changes, technology, disasters and weather, have formed our lives. Function follows the form and not the other way around.

The doctrine of change, the emphasis on the fact that all things are in transition, is an old and respectable one in philosophy. Five centuries before Christ, the Greek philosopher Heracleitus created a system of thought around the idea of continual change. Life, he said, is like a river. You cannot step twice in the same stream for new waters are forever flowing down upon you. This philosophy was put forth at the beginning of the Golden Age of Hellenic civilization when the Greeks were moving into the greatest climax of ancient history. It is especially significant today when we are concerned with the tremendous avalanche of new technology and a shrinking globe where we must somehow all live together. As we now know, no community in Western civilization is static and our communities are constantly changing as a product of our new technologies and our new life styles.

The classical view of history has for the most part examined events according to their political, military, and social accomplishments whether for good or ill. That such events have been motivated or caused by natural events, e.g. climate change, drought, etc., or by technological invention or discovery, has received little or no emphasis. In retrospect however, it becomes more and more clear that it was just such changes and events, weather, mechanical invention, etc. that have had the most profound effect on our history and even today are the main engines that drive our movements from the cities to the rural countryside.

Since the beginning of time right up to the 19th century, mankind with the aid of some very simple tools relied on his own (human) energy and the power of animals to shape his world. This primitive use of force and vitality was augmented somewhat by the power of wind and water in the 13th and maybe even as early as the 1st century, but by the end of the 19th and the beginning of the 20th century man's capacity for change increased by a thousand fold in transportation, communication, food production, manufacturing, the germ theory of disease and of course warfare and the development of weapons. The industrial revolution, like the Genie out of the bottle, provided man with an enormous increase in power and widened his horizons challenging even the most ambitious imaginations. But the ability to cope with these new found powers and advantages remained elusive and uncertain to say the least. Like the heated pressure in the boiler or the tea kettle, with the great concentrations of populations in the cities, the fragile economies and most importantly, the failure of the world's leaders to comprehend the complete impact of technology on society, only a spark was needed to ignite some of the greatest conflagrations of history, World War I and World War II. In the lull between these great wars as well as the years after World War II many of these pressures continue to build and grow to enormous proportions. Not the least of these is the increase in the populations of the world and in particular in the United States. In the next fifty years at the modest growth of 2% a year the U.S. will have a population of 669 million people. If the growth averages over 3% per year the population will be over 1 billion! Where will all of these people live in the 21st century?

The driving force for these changes, for good or ill, has been technology. Notwithstanding the inordinate passion of so many social engineers to "halt the urban sprawl" and/or "save the cities", the inexorable movement to the countryside continues with increasing momentum. That momentum is fueled with expanding technological improvements that the majority of Americans chose to take advantage of because it satisfies their desires and enhances their economic self interest. To recognize these trends and identify the important parameters that make up the composition of such movements is the purpose of this book. To accurately identify a problem is the first step toward its solution and/or avoid waste and provide for a smooth transition. A good understanding of these technological accomplishments along with the social dynamics that ensue can also provide us with some insight into the future so we can avoid much of the waste and mistakes which have burdened us in the past.

"Where there is no vision, the people perish: but he that keepeth the law is blessed." Proverbs, Chapter 29, Verse 18.

PART I

THE EVOLUTION OF CITIES

CHAPTER 1

URBAN ORIGINS

For the beginning of urban development we must look to the origins of organized agriculture and most significantly, the origins of metallurgy in the prehistoric world. Paleolithic and early neolithic homo sapiens was essentially a hunter gatherer and lived in relatively small groups since his food supply was limited to the distance a man could walk in a days time. If the group, usually a family, became too large, the food supply from this limited area would soon become exhausted and famine would fall on the family or tribe and they would all perish. The common practice therefore was to split the group when it became too large and then migrate to other hunting grounds. For more than 30,000 years this nomadic pattern avoided anything resembling an urban settlement. The beginning of agriculture dramatically changed this lifestyle. A dramatic change in the climate of the Northern Hemisphere took place about 10,000 years ago when the great ice sheets retreated from the northern continents leaving only those on Antarctica and Greenland. Soon afterwards, about 8,000 years ago, the warmest weather in this whole inter glacial period called the "Climatic Optimum" began. Temperatures ranged a degree or two higher than those of today. It was in this period that the agricultural revolution and our great civilizations began.

The earliest known agricultural communities probably developed only 10,000 years ago in present day Syria and Iraq along the valleys of the Tigris and Euphrates rivers. By at least 4,000 B.C. the cultivation of wheat and barley combined with the raising of goats, sheep and later cattle was spreading widely over southwestern Asia, northeastern Africa and Europe to effect this revolution in food supply we call agriculture. While most of these Neolithic settlements were still small communities of 20 or 30 households, they were more stable than those of Neolithic hunters and the agricultural economy afforded them time and energy for other activities including the new crafts of pot-making and weaving, as well as for the construction of durable dwellings.

As early as 5000 or 6000 B.C. members of the "Linear Pottery Culture" began to migrate north and west from their origins in the Carpathian Mountains in eastern Europe bringing with them a way of life based on cultivation. By 4500 B.C. they had reached the Paris basin. Archaeological digs reveal a culture based on sheep and cattle along with cereals and vegetables. These farmers built their farms and villages on the rich alluvial soil of the river valleys, e.g. the Danube, the Rhine, the Seine, the Oise and the Aisne rivers. Each village was made up of several "Longhouses" which had timber frames that were filled in with mud and roofed with reeds and grass. The longhouses were partitioned into three rooms with dirt floors. One room was for living, the second for food storage and the third was probably for animals. These houses were arranged in a crude circle with the farming of the land beyond the perimeter of the circle. This system lasted for a long time, but these settlements were not anything like what we call cities. By 3,500 B.C. some profound changes began to take place. Village development began to take place on the plateaus between the river valleys and fortifications (palisades and moats) and the production of weapons (flint arrow heads) were now commonplace. Warfare (defense) was now part of the culture.

Between 3000 and 2200 B.C. much drier conditions befell the ancient world and once very lush reaches of North Africa and Arabia turned to desert. Semitic people were driven out of the Arabian Peninsula into the Levant. Former inhabitants of the once-wet Sahara disappeared completely. After 2000 B.C. the climate changed again with the beginning of a cold spell and much wetter weather prevailed which undoubtedly reduced agricultural yields and increased competition for good land that could be worked with wooden plows.

As the middle and late neolithic age discovered the advantages of growing and developing agricultural crops for the comfort and assurance of a continuous food supply, the "need" for better and more efficient tools became more and more apparent. At approximately 4700 B.C. in the village of Vinca, on the Danube in present day Yugoslavia, some of these early farmers discovered and/or invented the process of producing pure copper from the natural surface outcrops of copper ore located nearby. Most recent discoveries have established this "town" as the earliest organized community to produce pure copper and copper tools. This was the birth of the "Copper Age". Most importantly, the very first use of the pure copper is believed to have been for personal adornment. The first copper scraping tools then followed and in a very short time the first metal weapons. The first gold ornaments have been found at the Black sea port of Barna not very far from Vinca on the Danube and have been dated at 4300 B.C.. These findings made for ornamentation and display predate Egypt, Sumer and Troy by 1500 years. These discoveries then place the seeds of our first urban centers at the onset of the copper age over six thousand years ago in the southeastern part of Europe during the Climatic Optimum. The town (Vinca) was made up of several one room houses arranged in a circle. Plots of land for the growing of crops were spread out on the periphery of this circle and the crude smelting furnaces were located a short distance away from this community center at the source of the copper ore. It should be noted that these recent discoveries predate the use of copper in the Nile valley at 3100 B.C.. Since copper is also found in the free metallic state and believed to have been used by neolithic man as early as 7000 or 8000 B.C., it was the discovery of reducing the ore to the metal by the use of fire and charcoal that really introduced the "Copper Age". Although this discovery also heralded the beginning of metallurgy, the use of the chimney which would develop a much hotter fire, was not known at this time. Correspondingly, fires for space heating and cooking in the houses were located in the center of the room with a hole in the roof for the smoke to escape. The true chimney was not appear in houses until the thirteenth century!

Prior to the beginning of agriculture obtaining food was really a very inefficient effort to scavenge from the earth whatever was available. As noted with the other primates and some primitive tribes today, this is not an effective way to live. Planting and harvesting crops, raising cattle and smelting metallic ores is an entirely different matter. Intellectual thought, organized effort and mutual consideration and communication is required to carry out the agricultural food production process along with smelting the ores, making the tools and building the facilities for storage of food and housing for shelter. After thousands of years of a rather moribund struggle for survival, mankind was now well started on the road to improve his lot and prevail over nature. Agriculture was the beginning of this improvement.

Notwithstanding this revolutionary improvement in mankind's food supply, cities as we think of them today did not develop for many centuries. Many of the qualities that we think of as civilized were attained by societies that failed to organize cities. Some Egyptologists believe that civilization advanced for almost 2,000 years under the Pharaohs before true cities appeared in Egypt. This period was marked by monumental public works, a formal state superstructure, written records and the beginning of exact science. This same type of development occurred in the New World too, although at a much later date. For all of its temple architecture and high art, and intellectual achievement represented by hieroglyphic writing and an accurate calendar, classic Maya civilization was not based on the city.

By 5500 B.C. it appears that the village farming community had fully developed in southwestern Asia. As a way of life it then stabilized for 1,500 years or more, even though it continued to spread from where it had first developed in the great river valleys. Then came a rapid increase in development. From the early villages serving the needs of the farmer and miner evolved the city. Subsistence agriculture prevailed for thousands of years before cities of any appreciable size developed. The largest social group was the village made up of no more than a dozen to maybe as many as two hundred households. Because this way of life was able to store food to avoid famine as well as having a fixed location of the village, the nomadic cultures who were still hunter gatherers, found them attractive and easy targets for their raids and predations whenever they faced famine or had to replenish their livestock or women. For over 2,000 years waves of Aryan barbarians, Kasites, Hittites, Cimmerians, Scythians, Medes, Persians, Dorians, Thracians, Celts, Germans, and Sarmatians, invaded the more cultured lands to the east, south and west of their northern homes. Sometimes they were driven back and sometimes they set up mighty empires.

Defense from these incursions soon became an important part of life for the subsistence farmer. Since the domestication of the horse on the plains of Poland

and the steppes of Russia, the Aryan Indo European nomads increased their ferocious raids with this increased mobility and the development of the two wheeled cart and the chariot. These early horses were not used as a combat tool since they were relatively small and it was too difficult for a warrior to remain mounted during combat without a stirrup. The stirrup was not invented until 150 or 100 B.C.! The only practical defense for the farmer was to assemble in larger groups, elect a war chief and fabricate the best weapons he could for his defense. This soon became expensive since weapons and defense preparations not only do not produce food, but the time invested could not be used for food production. The most dramatic development for these preparations was the city wall to protect the large assembly from the raiders. Initially these walls were made of mud bricks in the Mesopotamian cultures and where stone was available they were soon replaced with walls made up of the largest stones that could be moved into place. No mortar was used. The stones were dressed and fitted as tightly as possible although these walls were still sloped as were the mud brick walls which had to be sloped to maintain stability. The marauding nomads responded with improved siege techniques and devices and the struggle between the defender and the attacker has continued to this day.

Along with these defensive preparations came another burden for the farmer, "tribute or taxes" and the "draft". To build the walls, man the defensive positions, store the food and water for the people and the livestock and manufacture the weapons, all able bodied men had to contribute their time, skills and some portion of their grain and livestock. Since the farmer faced other problems along with defense, namely drought and/or flooding from the annual discharge of the rivers; canals, dams and detention ponds had to be built and maintained. No single farmer could cope with these problems, so great numbers of manpower had to be mobilized to complete these works and maintain the food supply for the people and the domesticated animals.

As food production increased and the cities grew, trade and commerce such as it was in these early times evolved with separate groups whose operations had nothing to do with the direct production of food or the mining of ore and the fabrication of tools. These new groups were made up of traders, artisans, religious leaders, scribes, soldiers and government officials. The nature of the services of this group was such that their location had to be reasonably accessible to the other groups of farmers, miner and individual land holders in any given region. Shipbuilding, pioneered by the Phoenicians, extended commerce and war throughout the Mediterranean and even beyond. There were two types of ships. The war galley, long and narrow with many oars and a small sail; and the merchantman, short and wide with few oars and a large sail. The sail was a single rectangular square sail. Most of the rowers were free workers and fairly well paid. The use of slaves and prisoners did not become common until the Renaissance! With addition of these groups to the village, especially if the village was a seaport, it soon became a city. In the next thousand years some of the agricultural communities on the alluvial plain between the Tigris and Euphrates rivers not only increased greatly in size, but also changed in structure. They culminated in the Sumerian city-state which covered the entire watershed of the rivers, with tens of thousands of inhabitants, elaborate religious , political and military establishments, stratified social classes, advanced technology and extended trading contracts.

Some scholars believe that the first steps toward the building of cities as we think of them today occurred with the building of temples for religious worship. A village selected for the location of such a temple thus became the focal point of gathering and worship for many of the farming villages in the region. Recent excavations below the ziggurat at Uruk, in present day Iraq, one of the first major cities, have also shown a continuity of worship from Ubaid times into the Uruk period of 4,000 to 3,200 B.C. These were the first people to develop writing, the use of numbers and measurements, including the beginning of the decimal system.

According to a great deal of archaeological work in recent years, the temple was an important part of many ancient cities. Along with the temple, defense played an important role for the urban center. Some early Sumerian mythology suggest the beginning of political institutions at this time with the assembly of the adult male members of the community to select a war chief to lead the defensive actions necessary to ward off the attacks of the nomadic tribes who were a continuous threat to the urban center with its relatively abundant booty at a fixed location waiting for the taking. Soon successful leaders were given a permanent job even during peace time and this appears to be the origin of kingship. As one might expect such developments led to the construction of defensive walls around the city. The early Mesopotamian king could trace his origin to the need for military leadership. With the advent of metallurgy then came better weapons including copper and bronze spear heads, swords, knives and with the introduction of manageable horses (although very small) from the steppes of Poland and Russia, the two wheeled chariot soon followed. The four wheeled wagon did not appear at this time since the wheels mounted to the axle could not make turns without skidding and dumping the wagon. With a fixed axle each wheel turned at the same velocity which could not work on a turning radius whenever the road curved. Technological improvements developed at a snail's pace at this time and it was hundreds of years before each wheel was mounted independently to the axle and the king bolt was introduced allowing the front axle to turn with the team. It wasn't until the wheels were mounted in this fashion to the chassis that the turn could be made effectively.

The general layout of these early urban centers included streets, unpaved and dusty, but straight and wide enough for the chariots and two wheeled carts, radiating out from the massive public buildings. These streets led to the outer city gates. Along the streets lay the residences of the well to do citizenry. These houses were usually arranged around spacious courts and sometimes provided with latrines draining into sewage conduits below the streets. Houses for the poor were located behind or between the large multi-roomed dwellings. These very small houses were served by small alleys and were not built as well as the larger houses. Merchants were probably located along the rivers adjoining the town or at the city gates. In these early times the central market place had not yet appeared. In other words, the function of these early cities was to provide for religious worship and common defense. Trading, politics, industry, banking, education or even entertainment had not yet become an important part of the city. Even though some of these urban developments were lacking, some of these sites were relatively large. The city of Uruk, in modern Iraq, covered over 1,100 acres and may have contained as many as 50,000 people!

Following very similar trends in development, ancient Jericho may well be the oldest town in the world. Palestine is an area with very little written history except for the Bible. Jericho fell to Joshua sometime between 1400 and 1250 B.C., but it had a long history before that. Excavations in recent years suggest that the town flourished 4,000 years before that time. Evidence from the digs indicates that the original settlement goes back to 8,000 B.C.. One most important feature of the location of Jericho is the continuous fresh water supply which prevails to this day. Even Jerusalem which David took from the Jebusites in 1,000 B.C. depended on a reliable water supply for its survival. The Jebusites had run a tunnel from the spring of Gihon, southeast of the city, to a natural cave beneath the city. They then excavated a deep vertical shaft from this cave to the surface so that women could lower their vessels into the reservoir. When David attacked Jerusalem, Joab led a party of Israelites up the shaft to capture the city. David then made him commander and chief. Water was very important for many reasons.

At about the same time that Jericho achieved the status of a town, the settlement of Hambledon Hill, circa 3,600 B.C.,in southwestern England reached a relatively high degree of urbanization with the construction of extensive fortifications and celebration of elaborate funeral rites. These accomplishments were the products of energies liberated from subsistence activities by the development of agriculture. Some evidence suggest that this town was demolished by warfare, but this is not yet clear.

Many other ancient cities developed, flourished and then perished in the time from 8,000 B.C. up to 1,500 A.D., but all following a similar pattern of development. Most of these were in the fertile crescent in the middle east but they also included Italy, Macedonia (Pella which was Alexander's home town), England, Russia and even the Mayan and Aztec cities in the new world in central America. The common denominator for all of these urban centers was the development of agriculture and a reliable water supply which provided the most important human requirement of a continuous water and food supply. Without these reliable resources, no time would ever have been available for the construction of the religious monuments, the fortifications or the manpower to maintain these facilities.

Many of these larger cities had to be abandoned whenever the rivers providing the primary water supply changed their course. This was especially true in Mesopotamia where the Tigris and the Euphrates run most of their course through very flat land and carry a great deal of silt. Once the silt deposits reach a critical depth, the next annual flood stage of the river will very often seek a new course. This problem is aggravated with the construction of levies built to control the flooding. The levies constricting the flow of the river during flood stage increase its velocity which increases the problem downstream and as is so often the case, finding a new course for its outlet. Although earthquakes and hostile attacks leveled many of the old cities, massive floods were probably the most devastating. Legends from the river valley cultures prevail even to this day. Ziusudra of the Sumerians built an ark to save himself and his family from a great flood sent by the gods. Ziusudra became the Utnapishtim of the Assyrians, the Noah of the Hebrews, and the Deukalion of the Greeks.

Along with the development of the urban centers also came the time for intellectual development. The Code of Hammurabi published in the 18th century B.C. is known as the first codification of laws regulating the lives and affairs of men. Hammurabi was the sixth and greatest king of the 1st Amorite dynasty of Babylon. The laws are inscribed on an eight foot high diorite stela which he erected in Babylon toward the end of his reign about 1,686 B.C. This code codified the many rules and regulations instituted by the Sumerians as early as 2,370 B.C.. The code touched almost all aspects of life and human behavior including identification of social classes, property ownership, labor relations, the family and criminal law with its penalties. Since both the Hammurabi and the Mosaic legislation include many provisions common throughout the ancient near east it is impossible to judge how much of the latter was dependent on the former.

Homer, circa 1,200 B.C., in ancient Greece, outlined his classic poems and epics which along with their historical accounts also brought to light the revelation that man's fate was not entirely in the hands of the gods and that he could save himself and improve his condition with his own ingenuity. And then to the Golden Age of Greece, circa 500 B.C., when extraordinary advances were made in art, literature, science, philosophy and democratic government. This was also the time of another climate change with increases in world temperatures. Warm and dry conditions also brought on droughts with crop failures in North Africa and trees and grass vanished from Lebanon and Galilee. Although it took a very long time from the beginning of the Agricultural revolution in 8,000 B.C., civilization had finally begun to improve itself and the seeds of progress were now well established.

Farming is very hard work, much more work than hunting or fishing, but much more productive Anything that could be devised to ease the burden of this toil or convey messages to the gods to improve production was in demand. Progress was very slow and did not spread evenly around the earth. Many cultures remained isolated because of natural barriers. The Sahara desert and the mountains of Ethiopia completely cut off the central African societies from any distribution of new ideas or technology. The Atlantic and Pacific oceans isolated North and South America, Australia and Japan.

The outstanding technological achievements in these early times were the many river engineering works needed for the irrigation of crops in the Nile, Tigris and Euphrates river valleys. The massive earth dams, river gages, canals and drainage of the swamps with the astronomical calculations to measure the seasons were testimony to the skills of these ancient engineers. In this same period knowledge of breeding and raising horses, domesticated edible animals and plants took place. Throughout this long time of development the production of a food surplus and the defense of person and family were the primary motives for supporting the first urban centers. The engine which empowered this progress was engineering and technology. These canals, dams, river gages, astronomical calculations, ships, pulleys, city walls, roads, chariots, carts and tools were the means by which the production of food was increased above the subsistence level. Without these improvements there would have been no surpluses to fill the storage bins, no reservoirs for fresh water supplies, no domesticated animals, no city walls or weapons for defense and no commerce or trade. In addition, there would have been no taxes since there would have been nothing to tax and there would probably have been no written language or codification of laws. Although traditional historical accounts cite the great leaders of the times as the primary reason for the great historical events, without these technological advances the events would have never happened.

Most of these ancient cities have almost completely disappeared although archaeology continues to shed more and more light on what they were, how they functioned and how they impacted history. Although they all had an agricultural economic base, trade and commerce stimulated their growth and military conquest and defense dominated their culture. Archaeological excavations show that the "city wall" was about the most prominent feature of the city with the religious temples and the palaces of the rulers occupying the central parts of the town. These excavations also give us some insight on the reasons why these cities perished. Again and again the destruction of the cities was by fire which along with some historical records indicate military conquest as a leading cause of the cities destruction. There are some important exceptions to this rationale. The Minoan culture on Crete flourished up to 1450 B.C. with practically no military defenses at all for any of the towns. The most dominant features of this society were the elaborate palaces, some covering two to three acres, and the impressive houses included in the highly developed towns, e.g. Knossos which covered about 185 acres. Minoan Crete had a rich export economy which extended throughout the eastern Mediterranean although most of this trade was with the Greek mainland. The evidence suggest that a major earthquake generated by a cataclysmic eruption of the volcano on the nearby island of Thera in 1450 B.C. destroyed everything on the entire island.

Another possible exception to the generalization of military conquest is the city of Pella in Macedonia. Although this city had developed very substantial fortifications and grew in wealth and power under Philip II, Alexander's father, when it was the most important city in the Greek world, it fell on hard times after the Roman conquest. It then suffered a terrible increase in malaria with the encroachment of its surrounding marshes and by the end of the first century A.D. it had virtually disappeared. Another exception to this generalization might be the Mayan Civilization of Central America. This culture whose origins may go back to the end of the last ice age, 8,000 B.C., reached it heights during the Classic period about 300 A.D. to 900 A.D and then collapsed. Notwithstanding the internecine warfare that may have restricted their progress, there is a strong suspicion that a major climatic change in the 8th or 9th century disrupted the basic food supply and precipitated the downfalls of the entire society.

Some of these ancient cities survived for thousands of years as long as there were no dramatic changes, e.g. volcanic eruptions, major climatic changes, hostile conquest or the depletion of a reliable supply of sweet water. If the city had been destroyed by hostile attacks then the new city walls, roads, temples and palaces were built on the ruins of the old structures. Jerusalem is a classic case. This city was originally a Bronze age Jebusite stronghold until its capture by David in 1,000 B.C. and remained the seat of the Jewish monarchy until its destruction by the Babylonians in 586 B.C. It was a prosperous capital again under the Herods just before the Christian era and then destroyed again by the Roman conqueror Titus in 70 A.D. Most of the walls that enclose the old city of Jerusalem today were constructed in 16th century A.D. by Suleyman the Magnificent. In each of these periods the new city walls and streets were built over and on top of the old structures.

In these earliest of times city planning was almost haphazard. The war chief usually drew a line with a stick in the earth to locate the wall at a respectable distance from the temple and then the streets, city wall, gates to the city and the palace, etc. found their locations accordingly. In the second half of the 5th century B.C. a famous town planner, Hippodamus of Milstus introduced the "invention" of regular town plans with a rectangular street system. The locations of the new cities at this time had changed from the river valleys of the Tigris-Euphrates and the Nile to the seaports of the eastern Mediterranean. In addition to the new rectangular layout, these new cities now included a market place at the center of the town. Temples and palaces were still located toward the center of the town along with the central market place which was now added. The market place soon became the weekly trading center for everything from vegetables, meat, pottery and baskets, pharmacy and dentistry. The size of the market place varied with the size of the town but ranged from 100 yards by 100 yards to 200 yards by 200 yards. The bakery and other more permanent specialty shops were usually located very close to the market square. The gates in the city walls led to the principle caravan routes or main highways away from the town. Shops and stores were still located outside the city walls, but many of them were now located inside of the walls too. As these urban centers became larger with the increase in trade and commerce many other additions were made inside of the walls. Government administration now required more facilities and barracks and stables along with storage of grain and hay for the horses were added. The police and soldiers now needed armories and the government needed meeting facilities for the officials and the general population. A forum was now added. The Greeks had introduced the theater to the world and now an open air theater seating as many as 500 to 1,000 people became the center piece for the cities. The fundamental requirements still were met, a reliable fresh water supply, streets wide enough to accommodate the horses and carts and special buildings to store the grain and hay along with the buildings for fulling the wool, baking the bread, pottery making, butchering the meat, tanning the hides and pressing the olives for the oil. A cemetery was usually located just outside the city walls. When the city was located on the coast, docks and quays lined the waterfront and the city wall would not enclose any part of the waterfront, but formed a semicircle around the rest of the city.

One such city, Leptis Magna, near Tripoli in present day Libya, may have reached a population of nearly 500,000 people 2,000 years ago when Rome dominated the Mediterranean. Traffic and manure became such a problem in this town that eventually all horses had to be corralled and stabled outside the city walls. Pedestrian traffic only was permitted inside the walls with the exception of the police and the fire department. With this arrangement over many years piles of manure accumulated to enormous heights of hundreds of feet just outside the walls. The manure would not decompose under the desert climate of the Sahara and are still there today! Human waste was also a problem and even though flush toilets were available in the bath houses, waste for the most part was pitched into the public street with the hope that it would be drained away when the winter rains drained the streets.

The design of the typical house in this period included a solid exterior wall with one or possibly two entrances, but no windows. Privacy and security were the main reason for this design. The house was built in a square configuration with an interior courtyard. All of the rooms faced the courtyard. Many of these houses were two story and could be very elaborate to satisfy all of the needs of wealthy people. Many times animals were kept in the courtyard along with attractive gardens and religious shrines. The houses were built with masonry walls and timber framing for the roofs which were very often thatched. Housing for the poor and/or the slaves was not as elaborate and were not much more than masonry or wood huts with dirt floors and a hole in the roof for ventilating the smoke from the cooking fires.

The houses were built along the sides of the streets which radiated out from the center of the town to the gates in the city wall. The market place, usually a large square, was located at the center of the town. The religious temples were offset from the market place as were the palaces, public baths and the government buildings. The government buildings were usually adjoining a large public forum in the Greek and Roman cities. The theater which often was the largest structure in the city was most often located on one side of town or the other. Small houses were located along narrow alley ways between and behind the larger houses. These houses were not much more than huts with no windows and dirt floors. Small shops for making and selling pottery, baskets, cloth, herbs and medicines, bread, etc., were generally located in the market place or as close to it as possible.

Although agriculture was the economic base for these communities, few if any of the farmers lived where their crops were raised or their livestock grazed. The olive trees, date palms, vineyards, fields of wheat and barley, cattle, goats and sheep were all located beyond the city walls and the farmer had to commute every day from the city to the fields and orchards.

Whereas technology in the river valley cultures was primarily devoted to hydraulic structures, e.g. levees, dams, irrigation ditches and the drainage of marshes, the technology in the Greek and Roman cultures extended to road building, bridges, stone cutting, flush toilets and radiant heating for the public baths. The Etruscans and the Romans introduced much more technology than did the Greeks. Rome relied heavily on its roads and bridges to hold its empire together. Without a doubt the Romans were among the greatest bridge builders of antiquity. One of the most significant contributions to this art form was their discovery of a natural cement called pozzolana. Along with this discovery was the development of coffer dams for building the bridge piers and most importantly, they brought the construction of the circular arch to the state of a fine art. One such bridge built over the Tagus at Alcantara, Spain carries the roadway 170 feet above the river and has stood for nearly 2,000 years. Bridges needed for military campaigns were built by the Roman legions, but most of the time the bridges were built by forced labor with the cooperation of the local townspeople. In these cases an engineer was sent from Rome to supervise the work and in this way the technology was spread over the entire empire. In this manner knowledge was spread and exchanged and the basis established for schools where professional standards were formulated. With these beginnings the art of building as described by Vitruvius evolved. One must appreciate how important bridges are to the development of trade and commerce and the growth and viability of any city. In any part of the world the land is divided again and again by rivers, creeks, canals, ravines and estuaries from the sea. Without bridges the movement of traffic and materials would be very limited and practically impossible for an empire as large as the Roman empire.

In reviewing all that we know of the towns and cities of the ancient world certain characteristics common to most all of these settlements stand out as the most powerful inducement for these people to congregate into the type of settlements we call towns or cities. The agricultural revolution enabled mankind to dramatically increase his food supply. After nearly one million years of just barely surviving by hunting and scavenging mankind was now able to produce food which not only provided for the family, but also provided for those who did not till the soil or tended the cattle. Now there was also a surplus. A square mile of fertile land with a good water supply could support up to 200 times as many people as before. Defense was one of the strongest incentives for these movements from the hills and valleys to the cities which also determined the configuration of the city and much of its infrastructure. The walls and gates, the food storage buildings, water reservoirs, the government buildings and the armories, all necessary for the defense of the community from the attacks of the nomads from the steppes and deserts of the ancient world. Religion and the development of doctrines for religious worship also contributed to the actual plan of the towns. As the high priest increased the complexity of the services necessary to placate the gods and protect the people from the ravages of the climate, pestilence and the raids of the brigands from the plains, the temples became larger and occupied more of the central cities. The development of technology too supported and nurtured the increased size of the towns. As more people gathered into the towns and cities better flood control and irrigation canals were required and more potable water was needed. This was therefore supplied from the dams and aqueducts along with better roads and bridges needed to accommodate the increased traffic from the horses and carts. One of the most significant technological achievements was the invention of writing and the first mathematical systems for counting and measuring.

Technology also brought its darker side with the improvements in siege weapons and cavalry equipment. With these new weapons and increased mobility alien armies destroyed many of the cities which did not have adequate defenses. Dramatic climate changes also devastated many of the ancient cities by eliminating essential water supplies. The agricultural economic base was absolutely dependent on a reliable water supply.

CHAPTER 2

CITIES IN THE MIDDLE AGES

The cities and living conditions of medieval Europe were much different than most of the descriptions that have been presented in many contemporary text. Many of these descriptions are really illustrations of Renaissance times in the 15th and 16th centuries. In the period commonly called the Middle Ages or the Dark Ages, circa 450 A.D. up to 1500 A.D., much of the splendor and glory of the more ancient and classical cities was gone and many of the ancient cities had disappeared altogether. The Roman empire which was at its peak about 2,000 years ago had practically ceased to exist as a world power by 500 A.D. Notwithstanding the authoritarian and other negative aspects of the empire, it did provide political stability, great advances in law, technology and even growth for the urban centers during its 1,000 year reign.

With the decline and break up of the empire, leadership and the focal point of urban business passed to the churches and the feudal lords with their small kingdoms. Most of the population lived in the country side. Only 3% to 5% of the population lived in or near the castles. These times were dark ages indeed. Population growth was minimal, learning and scientific knowledge which had been accumulated up to that time was confined to the monasteries. Roman aqueducts, harbors, roads and bridges fell into disrepair and ruin. Some bridges were even scavenged to build houses and churches, and some bridges were destroyed to isolate towns from marauding brigands. Literacy, which had been high under Rome, declined almost to zero and education was non existent except for the monasteries. Such science as there was became superstition. Religion was the common thread that held civilization together. This was the Age of Faith. The true city was not of this world, but in the after life. With this view point most people were more concerned with their salvation than with such mundane and prosaic problems as their roads, housing conditions or personal comfort. The gospel and Aristotle were the only doctrines of truth that one had to be concerned with to save their souls and understand the laws of nature or answer any other questions about life now or hereafter. Some of these religious practices went to the extreme. Pope Gregory I, called "the Great," burned the library of the Palatine Apollo, lest its secular literature distract the faithful from the contemplation of heaven.

This was not just an age of petty wars and robbery, but of famine and pestilence. Sanitary facilities were primitive to say the least and personal hygiene was unknown as a practical matter. Attila's ravages in North Italy were cut short by an outbreak of fever in 452 A.D. There was an epidemic of bubonic plague in 565 A.D. which was a major factor in weakening the defence of Italy against the Lombards. In 543 A.D. ten thousand people died in one day in Constantinople. Plague was raging in Rome in 590 A.D.. Pestilence was recorded in England in 664, 672, 678, and 683 A.D., no fewer than four in twenty years. Many cities of the east were left vacant and in several districts of Italy the harvest and the vintage withered on the ground. Were it not for the fact that most of the population lived in the countryside, Europe would have been decimated to its prehistoric population numbers.

A great deal has been written about the fall of the Roman empire, but one thing that most historians agree on today is that it was not "moral decay" and decadence that precipitated the fall. Actually by the third, fourth and fifth century Rome was Christian for the most part. The barbarians however played a more important role. Before 400 A.D. their incursions had been only destructive raids, but not fatal for the empire. But in 406 A.D. the Vandals invaded Gaul and headed for Spain at a time when the emperors of East and West were fighting each other to defend their borders. A few years later the Franks, Burgundians and others came in and settled and would not leave. A most important factor was that when these barbarians intruded on the empire, they learned the arts of peace and war which soon made them as formidable as the Romans. With the long frontiers of the Empire and the small population of barbarians, there never was a serious threat. But as the barbarian populations increased and their knowledge and power also increased, the long frontiers became indefensible. The barbarians not only learned from the Romans, but added their own inventive skills and knowledge. They invented soap and the barrel and built four-wheeled carriages. A Celtic native is believed to have invented the first harvesting machine. More significantly, the nomads who roamed the steppes of southern Russia and Turkestan invented the saddle and most importantly, stirrups were invented by the Samatians who roamed the plains north of the Caucasus. With these two inventions, the saddle and stirrups, the whole pattern of warfare changed dramatically. Instead of a contest of infantry and mounted infantry, a mounted and highly mobile cavalry entered the battlefield with devastating results for the traditional armies.

In Latin Europe neither political nor religious reform could sustain the old regimes of the Roman empire. The breakdown of public administration and the breach of the frontier led to a revival of parochial outlook and allegiance, but their focus was not on the city. Community life was now centered on the fortress or castle. Early medieval society was a creation of rural countryside villages and what remained of the old cities to meet the local needs of sustenance and defense. Communities were restructured into functional estates. What remained of the old urban centers was now viewed in this feudal and/or manorial organization. The distinction between town and country was now obscured when secular and ecclesiastical lords ruled over the surrounding counties as the vassals of counterfeit emperors or barbarian kings. The decline of city life in most of Europe was accompanied by provincial separation, economic isolation and religious other-worldliness. Not until the cessation of attacks by the Vikings and the Saracens would urban centers in Europe again experience sustained growth. Before the year 1,000 A.D. contacts with the rich Byzantine and Islamic areas in the Levant had revitalized the mercantile power of Venice which commanded the profitable route to the Holy Land during the crusades. Meanwhile merchant communities had attached themselves to the more accessible castle towns and diocesan centers in northern Italy and on the more traveled routes to the Rhineland and Champagne. They appeared along the rivers of Flanders and northern France and on the west-east road from Cologne to Magdeburg.

The focal point of the urban centers in these times was the feudal castle or the monastery. The city wall was still the most important defense system for protection from attacks from barbarians or more frequently, the neighboring city states in the region. In the community or just outside the city walls the houses were built in rows around the perimeter of their rear garden. Sometimes in large blocks they formed inner courts, with a private green which reached through a single gateway on the street. Free standing houses which wasted land were relatively scarce. Even the farm houses outside of the village would form part of a solid block that would include the stables, barns and granaries not too unlike the farm houses of the earlier Roman empire. The plan of the typical house varied with the region and the century, but certain features appeared common. A shop on the ground floor with access to the street and connected by an open gallery with the kitchen in the rear. The two rooms formed a court with the water well in the corner of the court. There was a chimney in the kitchen and in the living room or grand hall above the shop. From the living room there was access to the dormitories. The only form of an interior hallway was the open court which was necessary for the admission of light since there were no windows in the outside walls and there was no artificial lighting. The main plan for this kind of house lasted through the 17th century and even later. Depending on ones position on the economic scale the plan would be either constricted or expanded. The fact that the house served as workshop, store, counting house and residence eschewed any support for any kind of zoning as we know it today. The life style was very much family oriented.

The materials for the houses came out of the local soil which varied with the region. The earliest houses would have small windows with shutters to keep out the weather. Later these windows were glazed with oil cloth or paper. Glass did not come into general use until the 15th century and the initial quality was poor at best. Heating arrangements steadily improved. The open hearth in the middle of the floor, scarcely better than an Indian tepee, gave way to a fireplace and a chimney. With these technological advances combined with the increased use of distilled liquors for fuel the population steadily increased and the settlements of northern Europe expanded after the climatic changes opened up many of the alpine passes from the retreating glaciers. This warming trend started in the 4th century and lasted through the 8th, 9th and 10th century and undoubtedly helped increase the agricultural food supply for the population as a whole.

What gave the medieval town a sound basis for relatively good health was the fact that though it was surrounded by a wall, it was still part of the open country. Until the 14th century this was the prevailing demographic pattern. Even the old cities e.g. Rome, Paris or London were not heavily populated during this period. At harvest time the whole population of the town would go into the countryside to gather the crops for the winter's food supply. Hunters and fishermen would go to the fields and streams for the game and fish which was an important part of the local diet. It might be said that life style was more community oriented than it was in later times. The dwelling house was characterized by lack of differentiated space and differentiated functions. To compensate for this lack of internal differentiation however, there was much more complete development of domestic functions in public institutions and a corresponding dedication of open space not seen again until the 19th century. There were public ovens in the baker's shop, municipal bath houses, numerous public hospitals for people with diseases and for the lack of privacy in the congested dwellings, lots of open space in the "rye" for the lovers. Comfort and privacy were not part of medieval houses. Although sanitary facilities were to say the least primitive, this condition was not necessarily inimical to the health of the community. Using the animal dung heap for the family privy was much more healthy than using the contiguous river which at a later date was to receive the public sewer discharges and then provide for the public water supply. It must be remembered that the severe crowded conditions of European cities did not develop until after the Middle Ages.

The towns of medieval Europe were held together by the monasteries and the manorial lords of the local city states or kingdoms. These libraries of wisdom and knowledge, along with the entrepreneurial strategies of the barons who held the land, planted the first seeds of capitalism with their rent structures, market practices and trade policies. In the 8th century substantial changes began to appear which changed the thinking of town planning and over all economic policy. Global warming which began in 500 B.C. and lasted up to the 14th century had devastated North Africa and the Middle East with droughts, but substantially increased the growing seasons in northern Europe. Beginning early in the 8th century and for hundreds of years after, the Saracen invasions of Spain and the massive movement of the Vikings from the north into Ireland, Scotland, France, Germany and as far east as Constantinople from 795 A.D. to 851 A.D., Europe was caught in a military and cultural pincers movement that had a profound effect on its life style and the structure of its cities. In addition to the shock of the military attacks which the local population was totally unprepared for, of equal and perhaps greater impact was the hostile antagonism created by the confrontation from the two cultures which were alien to Christianity. Christian Europe labeled the attacks as savage, but to the Norsemen and Saracens, the destruction of all opposition was as normal as any other part of life. Europe was totally unprepared for such onslaughts either militarily or culturally. With the subsequent conquest, many defeats and immigration of vast numbers of the conquerors, the structure of the towns changed along with many value systems which the invaders introduced.

The cities soon found that the only reasonable defense against the onslaughts along the Atlantic and Mediterranean coast, the Rhine, the Elb and the Seine rivers, was to reconstruct and/or reinforce the old Roman city walls or to build new ones. With these alien invasions came new weapons to besiege the cities and the countryside. The Vikings with their shallow draft boats propelled by a single sail and very efficient single tier oars ravaged northern Europe with their raids. The Saracens brought with them new artillery which demolished the old city walls. The trebuchet invented in China between the 5th and 3rd centuries B.C. reached the Mediterranean by the 6th century A.D. and was one of the most instrumental weapons used for the destruction of the castles and city walls in Europe. The most powerful trebuchets could launch missiles weighing a 1,000 lbs or more with a range up to 250 feet. City walls could not withstand such attacks so extensive clearings were made outside of the walls and large earthen mounds or ramps were built to resist the barrages. The trebuchet was also used defensively, but this required a redesign of the city walls to include special square towers to replace the smaller round towers at the ramparts.

This great expense for defense with intensification of fears and anxieties ultimately turned back the invasions and set more of the stage for the beginning of the Renaissance. Of equal significance however, the change in the configuration of the city also set the stage for a more congested life style than had heretofore been the norm for the medieval town. These changes combined with the great improvement in food production from the technological inventions for the use of horse power and crop rotation severely increased the population densities of the cities. The invention of the horse collar increased the draw power of the horse so that cultivation of the soil was now meaningful compared to scratching the surface with a stick. Land that before was untillable could now be cultivated. The corresponding discovery that crop rotations would increase the yield added to the food supply which fed the increased populations of the cities. At the beginning of the 8th century the seeds of industrialization were planted in northern Europe. Water wheels to grind grain were located at every fast flowing stream in the northern part of the continent. Although the water wheel was known as early as the 1st century B.C., the scarcity of rapid currents and the great expense of constructing dams, necessary for the overshot wheel, severely limited the use of the wheel as a source of power in the Mediterranean basin. The abundance of slave power in the Mediterranean countries also reduced the need for any more efficient method for grinding the grain.

Although most historians record the beginning of the "Industrial Revolution" in the late 18th and early 19th century with the introduction of steam powered machines to displace manual labor, the process of industrialization actually began as early as the 8th century in northern Europe with the application of water power to the industrial process. In contrast to the Mediterranean drainage basin, medieval Europe lay in the drainage basins of rivers that flowed into the Bay of Biscay, the English Channel and the North Sea. In these regions there were hundreds of streams with regular flows which was most convenient for the development of water power. These natural circumstances combined with the social and religious pressures of chronic labor shortages and the great abundance of monasteries which required rigid adherence to schedules of work and prayer stimulated the development of the water wheel to unprecedented applications throughout northern Europe. By the late 11th century there were over 5,000 water mills in England and by the late 17th century there were 95,000 mills recorded in France although some of these were undoubtedly wind powered. In ancient times water power was used only for milling grain and sometimes raising water, but the flour mill was the most common. In medieval Europe social conflict developed when the feudal lords and the monasteries declared a monopoly on grinding grain within there own premises. In 1274 St. Albans Abbey at Cirencester, England, asserted a feudal monopoly of the milling in Cirencester and demanded that the townspeople surrender their querns. Fifty years later the townspeople attacked the Abbey with arms and extorted from the Abbot the right to own their own querns. A few years later the Abbot raided the town with his troops and broke all the querns. These quarrels over milling rights dragged on for centuries and some of these medieval monopolies were not done away with until the 14th century. The most significant advance in the use of water power was not so much in the wheels themselves, but in the uses to which they were put. The mills powered by water were applied to many task other than grinding flour. In the 9th century millwrights were grinding and polishing metal in cutlery mills. In the 14th and 15th century lathes were being turned, pipe boers, metal rollers with fans for ventilation and pumps for dewatering mines were some of the many applications of the "water wheel". The cam and the crank were developed by these medieval engineers during this period which expanded the application of this important source of power. The fulling and hemp industries were the first beneficiaries of these new applications and the paper industry soon followed. Production in the iron industry was always a slow and laborious process until the application of water power to the important processes of grinding the ore and operating the bellows to achieve higher temperatures for the smelting process.

The earliest water wheels were almost always mounted horizontally and were used exclusively for grinding flour. They were very inefficient, about 5% to 15% considering the dynamic energy of the water compared to the energy delivered by the wheel; and delivered less than one horsepower or about the power of a donkey or a horse. The vertical waterwheel was a substantial improvement and was built either as an undershot wheel or an overshot wheel. The vertical wheel played the most important role in the development of power in Europe and later on in America. The undershot wheel could be employed practically anywhere there was a water course and was the cheapest to build. The output was three to five times as great as the horizontal wheel, about two to three horsepower, and its efficiency was 20% to 30%. The overshot wheel was by far the best, but also the most expensive since it required a dam and an elevated water channel. However the overshot wheel could deliver up to 40 horsepower with an efficiency of 50% to 70%.

The steady numerical growth of water wheels was accompanied by geographical diffusion. From about the 13th century water wheels were turning throughout Europe from the Black Sea to the Baltic, from Britain to the Balkans, from Spain to Sweden. Within a couple of centuries even the New World received the benefit of water wheel power. Spanish engineers exploiting rich silver deposits near Potosi in the Bolivian Andes in 1573 built 32 dams by 1621. A main canal five kilometers long carried water to 132 ore-crushing mills near the city. The system generated more than 600 horsepower. It should also be noted that Spain delivered much more silver to Europe than the more glamorous gold bullion.

Clearly, the industrial muscle of the western world began with the use of the water wheel in Europe. The social impact was profound and especially important for the evolution of the city. The mills became the economic focal point of the region and in most cases the hub for the development of the municipality. It might also be said that the source of this natural power, the water way, was the central point of economic and population growth. Parenthetically, these focal points would shift when coal became the principal source of power in the 19th century! The focus would shift again in the 20th century when petroleum and electrical power became the primary source of energy.

Other significant advances in technology were made in this same period. By the 12th century the windmill was in common use in northern Europe and this improved use of natural energy also changed the economic and social fabric of the countryside throughout Europe. The origin of the windmill is lost in antiquity, but the early machines were not very efficient. By the latter part of the middle ages medieval engineers had improved the technology so that these mills were a significant tour de force in the economic production of food. One of the most significant advances for the development of urban centers was the invention of special rigs and developments of the lateen sail for sailing ships which enabled them to tack against the wind thereby making the ships independent of the direction of the wind and the efforts of the oarsmen. When William the Bastard crossed the English Channel to conquer England in 1066, he sailed in square-rigged ships which did not require oars. This profound advance in the art of water transportation portended a dramatic change in the development of principal cities in the world. The "Port City" from this time forward became the primary center of international trade, commerce and urban development. In this same period as has already been mentioned, the horse collar was invented. For thousands of years the horse had been at best a most ineffective producer of power because the yoke that was employed strangled the horse if he exerted too much tractive effort. In addition, without nailed shoes he often broke his hooves and became useless. In the ninth century however, the horse collar, which rest on the shoulder of the horse, was invented and in the tenth century the horseshoe along with the tandem harness was invented which allowed more than one pair of horses to pull a load. These innovations, especially the horse collar, increased the horse's capability as much as 400% and correspondingly increased food production on the farm with far less manpower. the result was a substantial increase in the number of people who could be supported in the city by the number of farmers in the country.

Water wheels, windmills, sails and horses, the original prime movers to replace man as the only source of power, combined with the efforts of the merchant elites seeking to free their communities from the heavy hand of the feudal lords and secure their governments to themselves, provided the greatest growth in the number of towns in history. By the 10th century the Vikings had discovered Greenland and even started colonies there. The Arab physician Rhoses had described infectious diseases, e.g. plague, smallpox, consumption (tuberculosis) and rabies. In this same period the Arabs brought arithmetical notation to Europe and in the year 1,000, the Chinese invented gunpowder. The first Crusade also started at this time (1091) and Europe suffered for hundreds of years from these incursions. With all of this technological ferment the stage was set for major social convulsions in Europe and especially for the development of cities.

No other event had such a profound impact on the cities of Europe and history of the world than the travels of Marco Polo. While Europe was still mesmerized with its goal to free the Holy Land from the Saracen, this young man with his father and uncle made a three and one half year journey to the court of the great Kublai Khan in China. Marco impressed the great Khan so well that in 1277 he was attached to the court and remained in China for sixteen years before he returned home in 1295. He was taken prisoner in a war between Genoa and Venice and there while in prison related the tales of his travels to a writer named Rusticiano. These stories stirred the imagination of all Europe, especially the tales of the gold in Japan and the millions of people in Asia. Along with the intellectual stimulation of Marco Polo's stories, Europe was also introduced to new technologies. Marco's travels were only the beginning of a considerable increase in the traffic between Europe and the far East. The traffic brought not only new ideas to Europe, but also extended the use of paper and printing from blocks which at the time was common in China. Gunpowder which had been invented in China was also introduced and of course the mariner's compass. The immediate result of the compass was to release European shipping from "coastal navigation" and dramatically expand commerce outside of the Mediterranean. Gunpowder which would soon eliminate the building of new castles in Europe was being used in primitive cannon and in 1313 Grey Friar Berthold Schwartz (Berthold the Black) allegedly refined the mixture of charcoal, sulfur and potassium nitrate (saltpeter) to the workable proportions of 1 to 1 to 3.5 and was then able to make a useable "thunderstick". These primitive weapons did little to alter the conduct of warfare since the guns could not hold a charge without blowing up and their accuracy was very poor. They weren't much better than the noise makers used by the Chinese who first discovered the gunpowder. The principal weapons of war were still the sword, the pike and the crossbow.

These great changes in the demography of the world and in the evolution of cities in this period would not be adequately described without considering the conquest of Timurlane (1336-1405). Born in Samarkand, a distant relative of Genghis Khan, Timurlane's rise to power over neighboring and distant tribes and kingdoms was accompanied by ruthless atrocities against any who resisted his claim to power. He occupied Moscow by 1382 and by 1385 all of eastern Persia had fallen to his sword. Iraq, Azerbaijan and Armenia had fallen by 1393-4 and Mesopotamia and Georgia by 1394. After suppressing many revolts with vigor, he marched on Syria and occupied Damascus in 1400. In 1401 Baghdad was taken by storm and 20,000 citizens were massacred. One legend has it that he built milestones of human skulls as a reminder of his eternal dominance over Iraq. Needless to say this devastating blow combined with the hostile climate and the expansion of deserts into the previously productive regions of the fertile crescent severely retarded any resurgence or healthy growth for the cities of the ancient world in the Middle East. In addition intellectual growth all but ceased. Since the Middle East had been the fountain head of knowledge for medicine, mathematics and metallurgy up to this time, the loss was terrible loss for the western world.

By the beginning of the 14th century the population of Europe, northern Africa and the Middle East had increased to about 100 million people. Without a doubt the new technologies, especially the horse collar and crop rotation, had increased the food supply and greatly expanded commercial trade. The increased trade between Europe and the far East traveled primarily along the Silk Road, the trans-Asian caravan route by which Chinese silk was brought to Europe. It is generally believed that this was the original conduit by which the great plague or the Black Death entered Europe in 1346. Along this route the trappers found an unusual abundance of dead marmots (a relative of the woodchuck) and skinned the carcasses for their valuable hides. The hides were then sold to the traders on the caravan routes. The first outbreaks occurred on the caravan stations on the lower Volga River in the towns of Astrakhan and Saray where the traders unpacked their wares for sale to the merchants. The plague carrying fleas then leaped from the dead hides to the warm blooded humans and the epidemic was well underway. The improved shipping and transportation facilities soon spread the epidemic throughout the Mediterranean basin and into northern Europe as far as Norway and England. After ravaging the populations of Denmark and Germany, the plague entered Poland in 1351 and Russia in 1352. All told this first great plague killed an estimated twenty five million people before it subsided.

By the time the Bubonic Plague had passed through Europe and the Middle East between 1347 and 1352 about one third of the population of the Western world had perished and the lives of untold millions more had been so seriously altered as to change the course of history. Neither the great or the powerful were immune. Eleanor, queen of Peter IV of Aragon and King Alfonso XI of Castile succumbed along with Joan, daughter of the English king Edward III who died at Bordeaux. The list went on and on. The Black Death caused the depopulation or total disappearance of about 1,000 towns and villages in Europe. The population of Europe did not again reach its pre 1346 level until the beginning of the 16th century. Some operations, such as the cessation of wars and the sudden slump in trade, followed immediately, but were of short duration. Many of the more serious economic consequences, e.g. the reduction in tillage and food production, the decline in rents, the ruin of the landowning classes and the rise in wages, proved the more lasting. There were many recurrences of the plague, notable during the years 1361-63, 1369-71, 1374-75, 1390 and 1400. The psychological damage was also very great. In the absence of an understanding of the germ theory of disease there was a general guilt feeling that this was God's punishment for a world which had been more interested in this world than in the next. Remorse and the constant fear of death dominated the entire population. Some historians believe that this period was the dividing point between medieval and modern history. The plague, fanatical crusades against heresy and Turkish encroachments on the routes to Asia worsened conditions in town and country alike. Europe turned in on itself. Except for a few large centers, activity in the marketplace was depressed; the cities surrendered their liberties and their ambitions. Without a doubt the "Black Death" impacted the history of the world and especially its cities more violently than any other single factor before or since the pandemic of the 14th century.

Toward the end of the middle ages certain characteristics of the changing urban scene began to appear as dominant forces which molded the pattern of living for people all over the world. Climate, conquest, disease, religion, natural catastrophes and technology had all changed the life of mankind. The typical response to all of these forces was to do anything one could to protect oneself and save his soul. The emergence of technology began to offer some hope that these forces, if they could not be conquered, could at least be stabilized and improve the lot of the people who survived the dark ages. The stage was set for the Renaissance. The spearhead for the Renaissance was technology. The compass was already expanding exploration on the high seas and block printing was spreading information beyond the walls of the monastery. Gunpowder now began to play a much more important role in the evolution of the urban centers of Europe and the Middle East.

It wasn't long before the first cannons came into general use. These first cannon were called bombards some of which were enormous. In 1453 at the siege of Constantinople the Turks used a gun that weighed 19 tons and hurled a 600 pound stone seven times a day. Constantinople soon fell to the Turks with this bombardment. After the Turks conquered the Baleen peninsula and Hungary, they besieged Vienna in 1529. The city wall was thin and fragile and there was no time to build a new one. The Emperor's general instead built a series of thick earthen embankments which absorbed the Sultan's cannon balls like a sponge. After a month, the Turks gave up and went home. The lesson at Vienna was learned well. Fortresses were redesigned with low profile and huge earthen ditches and embankments. The old time castle would soon become a relic of the past. The gun soon brought the feudal system to an end. What these huge guns did was to knock down the walls of the castles where the local barons had domineered the countryside and defied their king. By shattering the feudal castle, just as it had the walls of Constantinople, the cannon prepared the way for the era of kings who would rule by divine right.

The evolution of cities was heavily influenced by the development of weapons. One such development was the invention of the crossbow or as it was so often called, the arbalest. This simple hand missile weapon which probably originated in Italy very early in the Middle Ages was essentially a miniature version of the ancient Roman artillery piece called the ballista or engine of war. The crossbow shot a square headed bolt called a "quarrel" which was about ten inches long. The accuracy and range of this weapon was deadly indeed. Some of them had a range up to 300 yards! It could penetrate all but the heaviest armor and it was not long before the knight in his magnificent array of armor and expensive weapons became obsolete as the principal defender of the royal domain and more importantly the city and its supporting farmlands. The economics of defense were well illustrated with this technological change.

The expensive knight who could not as a practical matter be defeated (except by another knight) was the main instrument used by the royalty to dominate and control the merchants and the farmers in the kingdom. Without this means of enforcement taxes could not be collected, agricultural production could not be controlled and borders could not be maintained. Thousands of skilled hours went into the development of the knight which was certainly beyond the capability of any single peasant, soldier or combination thereof. The crossbow was relatively cheap and much more effective. It was so effective as compared to conventional bows, especially for piercing armor, that several popes declared that its use constituted an atrocity, except against infidels. Nevertheless, it proved to be the most effective hand missile weapon of the crusaders in their battles with the Saracens. Richard the Lionhearted won the battle of Arsuf (1191) largely because of the havoc wrought among Saladin's forces by the Christian crossbows. Practically all of the castle walls and the walls of the cities had been designed and built to defend against the conventional long bow along with battle strategies based on the location of fields of battle with armored cavalry supported by infantry armed with pikes and clubs. The crossbowman could fire from a prone position, with much greater range and accuracy and with much cheaper ammunition. Notwithstanding the superb accuracy of the English archers who had no equal in Europe, the crossbow was the weapon of the masses which eventually eliminated the knight as a major tour' de force in the city states of Europe.

The English longbow played an equally important role primarily because of its range, very rapid fire power and most importantly, its economy. Although the crossbow was very accurate and had a much greater range, it was very slow because of the heavy effort required to reload the quarrel. Therefore the use of the crossbow in open warfare was very limited (as compared to siege warfare) with this slow rate of firepower. The longbow was especially good on the open battlefield. The best and perhaps the most significant example of this superiority was the battle of Agincourt in 1415 when the French knights were devastated by the English bowmen with their longbows. With their horses shot out from under them, the knights tried to charge the bowmen on foot, but with the 75 to 100 pounds of arms and armor they got stuck in the mud and were slaughtered by the archers. According to some scholars this was the end of the knight as a significant power in the feudal system.

As mentioned earlier the Trebuchet invented by the Chinese and used so effectively by the Arabs played a major role in the redesign of city walls and completely revised the tactics of siege warfare. This devastating piece of artillery with an effective range of 600 feet was used up to the 16th century long after the introduction of gunpowder and the first cannon.

Weapons indeed altered the course of history and especially the design and construction of cities. As the new weapons systems developed, the cities had to change or perish.

CHAPTER 3

RENAISSANCE CITIES

The Renaissance and the beginning of world exploration are inextricably woven together. It might be said that the great age of exploration began with the expansion of the Turkish empire in 1453 when Constantinople fell and trade between Europe and the East was seriously interrupted. In 1526 the Turks held Buda-Pesth and had killed the king of Hungary. In 1529 Suliman the Magnificent very nearly took Vienna. The European city-states and countries were almost powerless before these onslaughts for they could not be organized into an effective resistance. Of the two principal rival cities of the Mediterranean, Venice was on much better terms with the Turks than Genoa. Every intelligent Genosese sailor fretted at the trading monopoly of Venice and tried to invent some way of getting through it or around it. There were now new people entering the sea trade and looking for new ways to the old markets since the ancient routes were closed to them. All over Europe merchants and sailors were speculating about new ways to reach the far East. The Portuguese put out to sea to the West and found the Canary Islands, Madeira and the Azores. In 1486 a Portuguese named Diaz, reported that he had rounded the south of Africa. A certain Genoese, Christopher Columbus, began to think more and more about the obvious, but which strained the imagination of the 15th century to the utmost, a voyage due West across the Atlantic to reach the far East. Although Columbus knew that the world was round, he grossly underestimated its size. Based on the travels of Marco Polo he thought that Japan with its reputation for great wealth would be his first landfall.

Spain became unified by the marriage of Ferdinand of Argon and Isabella of Castile and then set out to complete the Christian conquest of the last Moslem foothold in Western Europe. In 1492 Grenada fell. Columbus who was penniless, had failed to get support for his ideas from the Portuguese. He then appealed to Spain and shortly after the conquest of Grenada and with the help of some of the merchants of the town of Palos, Columbus got his ships. He got three ships of which only one, the Santa Maria, of 100 tons, was decked. The other two were open boats of half that tonnage. The expedition altogether numbered eighty eight men. Two months and nine days later at ten o'clock on the night of October 11, 1492 Columbus saw a light ahead. The next morning land was sighted and while the day was still young, Columbus landed on the shores of the new world, richly appareled and bearing the royal banner of Spain. He thought he had found India instead of Japan! Although he made several more voyages to the new world, Columbus died without ever knowing that he had discovered a new continent. The news of the new discovery spread quickly throughout Europe. The race was on. In 1522 Magellan was the first to circumnavigate the planet on his ship the Vittoria. Spain had found a new world abounding in gold and silver with wonderful possibilities for settlement and colonization.

In 1519 Hernando Cortez with about fourteen hundred horsemen and five hundred foot soldiers marched into the Mexican mountains and on to the Aztec city of Tenochtitlan where he was well received because the Aztecs suspected that he might be related to their white skinned god Quetzalcoatl. The Spaniards were amazed at what they saw. The city temples and public buildings were covered with hard white stucco that glistened in the sunlight and the main avenues were smoothly paved with a cement like finish. There were spacious market squares filled with goods ranging from jade and rubber to honey and vanilla. Flowers were everywhere. As they marched along the main thoroughfares they passed the fine houses of the Aztec nobles. The Spaniards estimated that the population was about 300,000 making it larger than the largest European city at the time. In many ways the Aztec capital was reminiscent of the ancient Sumerian and Babylonian cites for the architecture and the temple-pyramids were similar. Cortez and his men were astonished at what they saw for the Indian city was nothing like the dark, overcrowded cities that they were used to in Europe.

Farther to the South was the huge metropolis of Cuzco, capital of the Inca empire which included Peru, Ecuador, Chile and parts of Argentina. In 1533 Francisco Pizarro with less than two hundred troop sacked the city. A year earlier they had killed the Inca chief, Atahualpa in the city of Cajamarca after they had extracted a ransom of gold bullion that allegedly filled an entire room. Probably the most significant result of the discovery and conquest of the new world at the time was the rapid expansion of the supply of precious metals in Europe. When Columbus discovered America it is estimated that the amount of gold and silver in Europe was not over $400 million. By 1600 the volume of precious metals had reached five times that amount. Although some of it was plundered from the Aztecs and the Incas, the vast bulk of this treasure was silver mined from Mexico, Bolivia and Peru. The new wealth provided a mixed blessing. Whereas the new capital provided the seeds of the new capitalistic system, it also brought with it a substantial increase in inflation for Europe. Another result of the new discoveries of equal if not more importance was the introduction of new foods to European agriculture and the marketplace. Yams, maize, coco, tobacco, rum and most importantly, sugar (from sugar cane) were soon found throughout Europe and the Middle East.

The English and the French were not slow in following the example of the Spanish. The voyages of John Cabot in 1497-98 provided the basis for the English claim to North America and early in the 16th century the French explorer Cartier sailed up the St Lawrence thereby establishing a claim for France in the new world. The results of these voyages of discovery and the founding of the colonial empires are hard to overestimate. Commerce was now expanded from its narrow limits of Mediterranean trade into world enterprise. For the first time in history ships of the maritime powers now sailed the seven seas. The monopoly of Oriental trade held by the Italian cities of Venice, Pisa and Genoa sank into obscurity while the harbors of Lisbon, Bordeaux, Liverpool, London, Bristol and Amsterdam were crowded with vessels and the shelves of their merchants piled high with goods. Another change was the increase in the volume of goods and the different kinds of goods. Along with spices and textiles from the Orient were the now added potatoes, maize, tobacco, molasses and rum, cocoa, chocolate, quinine and cochineal dye from the new world; and ivory, slaves and ostrich feathers from Africa. The supply of older products, previously available in limited quantities was substantially increased. Sugar, coffee, rice and cotton were imported in such quantities that they ceased to be a luxury. This vast increase in the volume and scope of commerce along with the enormous increase in silver bullion was undoubtedly responsible for the growth of the capitalistic economy. The medieval idea of trade as an equal exchange was replaced by the concept of business for profit. Most significantly for the cities, the economic base for Europe had shifted from the Mediterranean cities to the cities off of the Atlantic coast. It should be noted here that this most important shift, from the eastern Mediterranean to the Atlantic coastal regions, did not happen because of any special political or military pressure or leadership, it happened because technology and new discovery had opened the way for the development and the opportunities that people wanted and/or needed to satisfy their ambitions and desires to improve their personal lives.

At this time Europe began an intellectual Renaissance which was long over due and now could create a more sound basis for the age of geographical and scientific discovery. Along with the new technologies of gunpowder, mining, printing and navigation some of the giants of science began to appear on the scene. Of these one of the most outstanding was Leonardo da Vinci. Da Vinci born in 1452 matured with the Renaissance as its most versatile figure. Painter, sculptor, philosopher, scientist, practicing Military and Civil Engineer, few were his equal then or even today. Leonardo deserves fame in the engineering profession however, more as a prophet than as a practicing engineer. Besides his machine guns, breech loading cannon, tanks, a submarine and a flying machine, Leonardo's sketches included lathes, pumps, cranes, jacks, water wheels, a canal lock, drawbridges, wheelbarrows, a diver's helmet with an air hose, roller bearings, a self-propelled carriage, a double decked city street, sprocket chains, an automatic printing press, a universal joint, a helicopter and a wooden truss bridge. There were many more devices as varied and as ingenious. His ideas were recorded on more than 5,000 sheets and drawings and notes. Unfortunately, these were scattered all over Europe in private collections and not published for centuries after his death. Other minds of the Renaissance indulged in much inquiry against the express warnings of ecclesiastical authority. It was a preposterous paradox that Christians got into great trouble with their church when repudiating the ideas of the great pagan Aristotle, but apparently this was the case. The trial of Galileo before the seven cardinals in 1653 would be a comic opera today.

Except for the paroxysm resulting from the new ideas conflicting with the old traditions, Galileo properly pointed out the fallacies of Aristotle's statements that the velocity of a falling body depended on its weight and that there were two kinds of motion, natural and violent. From his experiments Galileo demonstrated that there was only one kind of motion; the forces that caused the motion might be different, but not the motion itself. This important study also revealed to Galileo that Aristotle had been wrong about the motion of the earth and that the Polish scientist Copernicus was correct when he wrote in 1543 that the earth revolved about the sun, not the other way around. The Church was not able to accept this challenge to Holy Scriptures concerning the relationship between heaven and earth. And so it went with this new thinking of the early Renaissance, things were not what they might seem to be and careful experiment could reveal the truth. Stevin the Netherlander, 1548-1620, developed his "parallelogram or triangle of forces" which established the science of statics. From this discovery evolved the new design of bridges, large buildings, and eventually, large municipal sewer systems. Other great discoveries soon followed. Galileo's secretary Torricelli made a quantum leap forward when he discovered that the pressure of water was proportional to its depth. Later Pascal together with Torricelli developed the barometer which exposed the fallacy of Aristotle's belief that nature abhorred a vacuum. Then Fermat, 1601-1665, and Descartes, 1596-1650, independently discovered analytic geometry which measured the relationship between such variables as temperature and pressure, speed and power and countless other groups of variable quantities. Others of no less importance made their great contribution during this period of great revelation. Boyle, 1627-1691, with his famous gas law; Hooke, 1635-1703, working with watch springs developed the famous law which bears his name, namely, that up to the elastic limit materials respond to tension or compression in proportion to the load put on the material. Hooke also developed the universal joint which had been suggested by da Vinci. One of the greatest of this group was no less than Isaac Newton, 1642-1727, who laid down the principles of uniform motion in clear and unequivocal terms. These laws have since become the basis for all of the design of machines and operating parts up to the present nuclear age. Along with this great advance came the invention of the differential calculus by Leibniz, logarithms by Napier and the slide rule by Oughtfred in 1622.

The technology of printing made enormous strides in this period. Books of almost every subject multiplied after Gutenberg's bible had appeared in 1454. The notes on construction of the Florentine architect Alberti, 1404-1472, had accumulated for thirty years before they were published in 1485. During the following years the works of Vitruvius were published and relying on this work. John Shute produced the first book on Architecture in the English language in 1563. Biringuccio's work on metallurgy was published in 1540 and in 1556 the more widely known work on mining and metallurgy by Bauer was published. The publication of many more books began the wide dissemination of important scientific, technical, literary and political knowledge throughout the western world. The light of the Renaissance began to cast its light to the far corners of the entire world.

The new scientific insight and the subsequent explosion of knowledge began its impact on the world in Europe and its urban centers. Bridge building, an important key to urban development, underwent substantive changes and improvements. Although travel and commerce did not stop altogether in the middle ages, bridges were scarce and the old Roman roads were badly neglected. In some parts of Europe bridges were actually torn down to give communities the natural protection of their river barriers. Bridge builders in the middle ages gave little thought to the strength of the materials of their construction and then piled on houses, shops, towers and other superstructures of all sorts on the bridge decks. It was not long in these cases before the ravages of fire, floods, extreme frost and heavy snow destroyed these important focal points of transportation. The new Renaissance scientific and engineering thinking changed the art of bridge building. Aandrea Palladio, 1518-1580, is believed to be the first to introduce a bridge truss in 1570 across the Cismone

River near the border of Italy and Germany. Bridges such as this with lighter, better wood materials and longer spans to clear river traffic soon appeared throughout Europe.

For the cities of Europe the results of the age of discovery provided a mixed blessing. Along with the enormous increase in food production, trade, introduction of a new economic system and the great influx of silver and gold bullion, population density in the cities increased beyond all previous limits. By this time no new cities were being formed in Europe and the congestion in the older cities ended the Medieval standards of building space. The structure of the cities had become substantially altered with the influx of wealth and the patronage of the Baroque palaces. The old feudal aristocracy had become urbane. Thanks to aristocratic patronage, the theatre took on its modern form in London, Paris and the minor cities. The Baroque orchestra had been formed taking music out of the home and into the public theatre. The outstanding art museums of the world were now formed at the Vatican, the Louvre and the National Gallery to house the fruits of conquest and the treasures that were purchased with the new wealth. The municipal park and in some cases the zoo, had now become an important feature of the city providing an equivalent of the smaller pleasure grounds and playing fields of the medieval city.

But the new look of the cities ignored the problems that accompanied the increased population density. Land values increased and the slum became the characteristic mode of the 17th century. The science of sanitation was unknown and with the increased density there was an enormous increase in the morbidity rate. The Bills of Mortality of London in the 17th century, which were the vital statistics of the day, indicate that the death rate in large cities at that time was greater than the birth rate. The growth of the cities was due entirely to migration from the country to the city.

In America the formation of new cities became a matter of convenience to the prevailing commerce of the day. Ports of entry, good harbors and good access to the systems of river transportation were the primary criteria for the location of the new towns. Along with the requirements of commerce and trade, the strategic location of some of these communities qualified them for the addition of military forts which were necessary to defend the various interest of the competing claims made by the countries of Europe. In each case the planning and structure of the town followed the style of the country in Europe from where the settlers had originated. The outstanding difference was the growing alienation to the political and economic dominance of the European monarchies over the American cities.

Although the Baroque period, from the latter part of the 16th century to the latter part of the 18th century is more well known for its curved architecture with terra cotta figures, the paintings of Rubens and the music of Bach and Handel, the cities of this time underwent many profound changes. Gunpowder with the improved technology of field artillery had made the old walled cities and castle fortifications totally ineffective. The telescope discovered in Holland in 1608 and perfected by Galileo in 1609, expanded the range of artillery which now made the castles historical relics. Power was now consolidated into the larger towns with newly designed walls and better defenses against the non-explosive artillery balls.

Instead of the simple masonry wall, which an ordinary house mason could build, it was necessary to create a complicated system of defense that called for great engineering knowledge and a vast expenditure of money. These new fortifications, difficult to build, were even more difficult to alter except at prohibitive cost. They put an intolerable burden on the municipality and brought to the city the exorbitant aid of the financier. But equally disastrous to the life style of the population was the impact of the new city plan. While the old fashioned city was divided into blocks and squares and then surrounded by a wall, the new city was planned as a fort and the city was placed in a straight jacket. The opportunity for horizontal expansion was over. New growth could take place only in the vertical direction. No prudent man would build his house outside of the new city walls. In fact this area just outside of the city walls was usually kept cleared as an added defense against the long range artillery. Not only did the new fortifications remove the suburbs, gardens and orchards too far from the city to be reached conveniently, but the open spaces within the city walls were soon built over as the population was driven from the outlying land by fear and disasters from the marauding brigands. The overcrowding of the cities increased setting the stage for more disasters. The increased population density without proper sanitation was the creation of one disaster after another just waiting for the happenings. And indeed they did happen. Cholera, typhoid, dysentery were the main visitors to these population centers and the people were helpless and terrified as they buried their dead.

Along with these changes and the multitude of wars that accompanied them, the standing army became commonplace. War now became a continuous activity instead of an intermittent or spasmodic occurrence. In an economic crises the guns, of the professional soldiery could be turned against the populace at the first signs of revolt or failure to pay the taxes. The standing army recruited for permanent warfare became a new factor in the operation of the city state and the capital city.

The town itself did many things which in modern times are done by the state. Social problems were taken up by the town administration. The regulation of trade was the concern of the guilds in agreement with the council, the care of the poor belonged to the church, while the council looked after the town walls and the very necessary fire brigades. The council mindful of its social duties tended the filling of the local granaries in order to have supplies in the years of scarcity. The town was also the chief capitalist. As a seller of annuities on lives and inheritances, it was a banker and enjoyed unlimited credit. In return it obtained means for the construction of fortifications. For the most part these European towns were independent or quasi-independent aristocratic republics which admitted a vague overlordship on the part of the church or the emperor or the king. Others were parts of kingdoms or the capitals of dukes or kings.

The applied technology of the Baroque period was pretty much limited to the newly discovered principles of structural engineering and the increasing use of the mariner's compass. The science of statics first outlined by Jordanus de Nemors in the 11th-12th century, refined by da Vinci, 1452-1519, and published by Simon Stevin, 1548-1620, with his triangle of forces in 1585, permitted the analysis and subsequent design of the Baroque buildings which spread over Europe to supplant the older Gothic structures. The new structural design techniques permitted the construction of the new more complex city walls which were designed to defend against the new and improved artillery. These new fortifications had outworks, salients and bastions in star like formations which permitted the artillery and the armed infantry to rake the ranks of the attacking forces from whatever side they might approach. In effect, the defenders could now protect the city away from the central core of the city. These ingenious defenses seemed to promise security, but the economic burden to the community was enormous. Urban design based on these Renaissance principles remained essentially unchanged throughout the 17th century although Fontana's meaningful emphasis on communication routes and gathering spaces became the model for most later large scale urban designs or renovations. Most importantly, with the newer designs and the tremendous increase in population density, there were no improvements in sanitary facilities.

With the seeds of capitalism well established in Europe, there was a great increase in trade for the cities. Whereas the previous economic effort of the city-states had been for the most part very provincial, the new method of operation was to receive the imported cargoes from the new overseas sources, distribute the goods to the towns and manufacturing centers and in turn ship and distribute the manufactured finished products to the foreign markets. Canals were now constructed on a scale heretofore unknown in Europe to improve the efficiency of this new type of commercialism. Italian, Flemish, Dutch, and French engineers were digging canals with an earnestness that is best described as patriotism. Their sites were strategic and their economic purposes national in scope.

The technical development of the Dutch city was based on the marvelous control of the water, not merely for the communication and transportation, but for the sculpture of the landscape, established by the Dutch engineers. Their influence was felt throughout Europe. This command of water had a tremendous impact on the city. It gave the Dutch city not only a clean facade, but a super-clean interior. The big windows of the 17th century small house in Holland brought an unprecedented amount of light and air into the interior that undoubtedly lifted the spirit and opened the mind. These layouts are to this day still above the level of a good share of modern housing. No less outside the baroque framework was another phenomenon of the 17th century, the New England village of America. The center of the village was an open common, dominated by the meeting house and the town hall. These three institutions served as the focal point for the community. The common also served for military drill as well as the pasturing of the cattle. Around the central area were the separate houses, sometimes a single line on a block, with deep rear gardens large enough for a small orchard as well as a vegetable plot.

In the 17th century the great capitals of Europe had begun to absorb population with no effort at limitation, but in the New England town of this period there was no growth except for the absorption from its members. When near crowding, a new congregation would move off under a special pastor, erect a new meeting house, form a new village and lay out fresh fields. Hiving off to new centers discouraged congestion in the old ones and the further act of dividing the land among the members of the community in terms of family need, as well as wealth and rank, gave a rough equality to the members. Each family had its rights in the common lands; each family had fields on the outskirts as well as the gardens near their homes; each male had the duty of participating in the political affairs of the town through the town meeting. A democratic setting which was the most healthy of urban environments; a typical contrast to the despotic order of the dominant baroque city of Europe.

While the architects and engineers of Holland as well as the pastors and governors of New England made magnificent strides in the style of living for their cities, the rest of Europe was struggling with the congestion and squalor of their capitals and striving to improve their productivity to capitalize on the new commercialism. A major part of this effort at this time was devoted to dewatering the mines with very inefficient pumps. Iron and coal were beginning to dominate the economy, but the pumps driven by horses could not keep up with the copious amounts of water in the mines. In 1698 the first steam driven pump was introduced by Thomas Savery, but because of its cumbersome operation its use was very limited. Savery's invention however started the great movement toward the use of fire and steam. Thomas Newcomen then introduced the first effective steam driven pump in 1712 and the age of steam was really started.

Early craftsmen had discovered that for producing iron from iron ore there was no fuel as good as charcoal. Wherever the industry took hold, charcoal burners ruined the forest of the land. It was this calamity rather than the success of the early ironworkers which led to the next great advance in metallurgical engineering and hastened the introduction of the steam engine for the industrial age. The smelting of iron by the use of coal has been credited with having as much historical importance as the Norman conquest of England, King John's signing of the Magna Carta, the discovery of America by Columbus or the defeat of Napoleon Bonaparte. The day in 1709 when Abraham Darby actually smelted iron ore with coal on a commercial scale was a day of revolution not simply in metallurgy, but a major factor in determining the subsequent history of Britain and in fact the world. Admirals and statesmen were alarmed for the future of the Royal Navy and British supremacy on the high seas if their oak timber supply was destroyed. The government had done everything for years to encourage the production of iron with coal.

No invention since the introduction of gun powder to Europe was to have such an impact on the cities of western civilization as the steam engine. James Watt's improvements on the Newcomen steam engine were so profound that today he is given credit along with Savery and Newcomen for the invention. Watt included a separate condensing tank connected to the cylinder but still separated from it. He made many other improvements including the use of steam instead of atmospheric pressure to push the cylinder down. With these and many other improvements the Watt engine saved three fourths of the fuel which was required for the Newcomen engine. The Newcomen pumps and the improved Watt steam engines were soon spread over Europe primarily for use in dewatering the mines. The demand for the engines soon exceeded the ability to produce them. When John Wilkinson patented the first cylinder boring mill in 1774 in England, the efficiency and production of the steam engine was again improved with the additional application that had now become available. Wilkinson pioneered in applying steam power to the rolling of iron. He was also the first to launch an iron ship in 1787. It was a barge 70 feet long built of riveted iron plates. The synergistic effect of this great invention, the steam engine, was indeed profound. It changed the way people lived their lives. Steam penetrated rapidly into the established industries of milling flour, sawing wood and stone, pumping water, hoisting coal, mining and crushing ores, smelting and forging iron. Most significantly, with the use of the steam engine these operations no longer had to be located near or at a water fall on a river. The textile industry soon adapted the new source of power to its production facilities and England was now the leading industrial center of the world and would remain so until the 20th century when it would be overshadowed by Germany and the U.S.A. At the beginning of the 19th century the baroque style of planning was the image of order for the cities, but the shadow of the industrial revolution was now being superimposed over this plan.

Although most historians credit the Renaissance with great awakenings in art, architecture and literature and with very little change in the general make up of the towns and cities, a closer examination reveals some very substantial changes in the structure and composition of the towns and cities of Europe. The mariners compass and the new rigging for sails allowed the new age of discovery to literally reshape the world. Population growth and the development of new cities shifted from the eastern Mediterranean to the coast of the Atlantic. The new sciences of statics allowed new and better bridges to be built and the houses in the cities now increased their size to three and four stories to accommodate the increased populations. Gunpowder and the new cannon reshaped the city walls. The printing press of course changed all thinking for the development of engineering and science and set the stage for the industrial revolution of the 19th century. One of the most significant changes in the structure of the towns and cities of this period was in the development and expansion of public water supplies. The relationship between "bad" water and disease had long been recognized, but never understood. As the density of the towns increased the local wells became more contaminated from the animal refuse and the residential outhouses. This problem caused many municipalities to build aqueducts and some ingenious mechanisms and devices for lifting water from the rivers for distribution in the wood and lead pipes to the neighborhoods. One of the most famous of these was the system which Peter Morice built for London in 1582 when Elizabeth was Queen. Morice made use of the power of tides that were sweeping through the narrow arches of London Bridge. His undershot wheels generated more than 100 horsepower and ran ten piston pumps that raised 4 million gallons daily through a 12-inch main to the height of 128 feet. From the reservoirs the water flowed by gravity through lead pipes to the houses of London. Similar improvements took place in these times in Paris, Augsburg, Germany, and Toledo, Spain.

These technological developments not only changed the cities, they changed the entire world. The cities increased their population densities to unheard of limits and the water born diseases now began to take their toll. Without the understanding of the germ theory of disease and the increases in population, the morbidity rates escalated to new heights and the mortality rates increased dramatically.

By 1600 Europe's population had increased to over 63 million and American cities were starting to develop following the patterns set down in Europe. Santa Fe, New Mexico became the first capital city in America in 1605. In 1636 Harvard College was established and in 1639 the first printing press in North America was started in Cambridge, Massachusetts. By 1680 the population of the American colonies was estimated at 155,000. Most of these people were in New England and Virginia. The rest of the North American continent was one vast wilderness. In 1687 Sir Issac Newton published the Philosophiae Naturalis Principia Mathematica in which he established the laws of motion and gravity. This became the foundation of modern science up to the nuclear age. At the beginning of the 18th century, 1700, the population of America was estimated at 275,000. This did not include Indians. Technology was not helping much to ease the pain of disease and natural disasters that still burdened Europe and the rest of the world including America.

The slow pace of technological improvements was especially troublesome in America at the beginning of the century. Development of any kind was hard and time consuming. The immense forest with mountains, deep, wide and fast moving rivers as well as not too friendly Indians, all militated against any rapid expansion into the heartland of the new world. Tools and equipment for clearing the land, building the roads and bridges as well as the houses, barns and fences, were primitive and labor was always in short supply. Horsepower and human muscle were the main ingredients of any development whether for the farm or for the city. Most of an individual's time still had to be spent on growing, preserving and preparing food and fodder for the family and the animals before any spare time could be spent working the land for future development. In the absence of knowledge, science and/or technology, life styles and the standards of living hadn't progressed much since the Middle Ages.

Europe's quarrels and the bitter disputes between religions exacerbated these problems in America and the French and Indian wars offered little relief for the life of the colonial farmer trying to scratch out a living from the stubborn land. Actually the Europeans didn't consider North America that great a prize since the colonies weren't that profitable. England tried to confiscate all of the "tall timber" for her naval stores and the French wanted the fur trade, namely the beaver pelts, but other than these and some excellent fishing off of Nova Scotia and Newfoundland, America didn't have that much to offer any European investor. The West Indies in the Caribbean were a very different matter. Here was a prize that was envied by all: Sugar! Sugar was king in Europe and whoever controlled Jamaica, Cuba, the Dominican Republic, etc., would reap the profits from this new world bonanza. The French and British fleets sparred continuously all over the Atlantic for this control and the sea ports from Boston to Charleston were very important for this struggle.

With the cessation of the French-Indian wars, the British took undisputed control of the New World and sought a way to pay for the long and expensive war they had fought with the French. Parliament and King George thought that the American colonist should bear the burden of this cost and levied the taxes accordingly. The response from the colonies was an overwhelming No! The main reason for this objection was the fact that they, the colonist, had no representation in Parliament and since they were British citizens, they believed this to be unjust and refused to pay the tax. Over the years the dispute heated up with both sides digging in their heals. When the British General Gage was ordered to go to Concord to search out and confiscate all the muskets and powder from the houses and public buildings, the word went out from Boston via the underground telegraph, Paul Revere, that the "Regulars" were coming. At Lexington, on the road to Concord, the American Minute Men assembled with their muskets to intercept the British troops. At this encounter, the "Shot that was heard 'round the world" started the American Revolution. The troops easily cut down the Minute Men and proceeded to Concord where they confiscated very few guns. On their return to Boston however, the British troops met resistance like they had never before encountered. They suffered very heavy losses. One of the main reasons for these losses was the inferiority of the British musket, 'Ole Bess. The musket had a short range, was inaccurate and the troops were not well trained for shooting. The British army relied much more on the bayonet and looked upon the musket primarily as a means of mounting the bayonet. The poor quality of this musket was a handicap for the British throughout the war. The colonist for the most part had French made muskets which were much more accurate and had a range two to three times that of 'Ole Bess. This superior musket was not very good with a bayonet however, and whenever the colonist engaged the Brits with bayonets, the better trained regulars almost always beat the colonist. The colonist capitalized on their superior weapons technology by using Indian tactics of warfare with camouflage (no red coats) and surprise attacks. The British suffered heavy losses on their retreat from Concord to Boston and especially at the battle of Bunker Hill (Breed's Hill) because of these inferior weapons and failure to understand the Indian style of warfare. The war went on for eight years before a peace treaty was signed in 1783. The United States now faced the formidable task not only of recovering from the war damages, but also trying to grow and expand into the wilderness as they faced the beginning of the 19th century.

CHAPTER 4

CITIES IN THE INDUSTRIAL AGE OF AMERICA

Technology proceeded at a slow pace in America in the 18th century. A census taken the year after Washington's inauguration in 1789 showed that the country had nearly four million people of whom about three and a half million were whites. This population was almost entirely rural. Only five cities which were major urban centers existed: Philadelphia with 42,000 people, New York with 33,000, Boston with 18,000, Charleston with 16,000, and Baltimore with 13,000. The great bulk of the population lived on farms and plantations or in small villages. Communications were poor and slow, for the roads were bad, the stagecoaches very uncomfortable and the sailing vessels sporadic and unreliable. Most people lived isolated lives with poor schools, few books and only occasional newspapers. What was almost completely lacking throughout the country were any of the technological tools and facilities that were commonplace in Europe at the time. Anything of metal that was cast or machined was made in Europe. Except for the most simple home spun, good clothing and fabrics were woven in British textile mills. It is noteworthy that in 1769 a French military engineer, Nicolas Joseph Cugnot, built the first automobile. It was powered with a steam engine! Sales weren't overwhelming, but it was a harbinger of things to come.

Living conditions in rural America were at the subsistence level at this time with practically all of ones waking hours spent in the production and preparation of food for the people and the animals. The work was hard for men and women. Backbreaking toil was required to clear the land, mill the timber, build the barns and houses then collect and prepare the food and fuel for the long winters. Only the most rudimentary tools were available for these task and most of these were made by hand or imported from England. Hardship, disease and poverty took a heavy toll. Other perils included Indian warfare, malaria, wild animals and, of course, the roving bandits.

This condition soon began to change. Turnpike companies began to be formed and a model road was soon made from Philadelphia to Lancaster. Canals were dug and most importantly, immigration from the Old World began to come in such volumes that at times many people thought that half of western Europe was moving into the land. Washington especially liked the idea of bringing expert farmers over from Britain to teach Americans better agriculture methods. The rich soils of the Mohawk valley in New York, the Susquehanna in Pennsylvania and the Shenandoah in Virginia soon became the finest wheat growing areas in the country.

Manufacturing was growing too. Massachusetts and Rhode Island were starting textile industries and Connecticut was starting to turn out tinware and clocks. The Middle States were turning out paper, glass and iron. But no mill towns had as yet appeared with their populations devoted exclusively to manufacturing. Most of the manufacturing was still done in the homes. Coarse cloth, leather goods, pottery, iron implements, maple sugar and lead bullets were the common products. When the mills and factories did spring up, the owner most often labored alongside his hired hands in the shop. Shipping was also developing with emphasis on costal shipping although in 1787 American ships were trading in Canton, China! The main movement of the country was westward, ever westward.

Up the long slopes of the Alleghenies the emigrant trains climbed in their white topped Conestoga wagons. Through the Cumberland Gap came the hunters and the pioneers with their carts of furniture, seeds, animals and simple farm tools. Each year the Ohio and the Mississippi saw more rafts and barges floating down to New Orleans with grain, salted meat and potash. The western towns of Cincinnati, Nashville and Lexington grew larger and more important. One of the most important characteristics of these towns was there location on the transportation arteries that existed in the eastern United States. As the country entered the 19th century, technology originating in the United States and Europe began to change the destiny of the United States and the world.

In 1795 Robert Fulton invented the Power Shovel which was to be used in digging canals. In 1796 Edward Jenner, an English physician, issued the first smallpox vaccine to a boy with matter from a cowpox lesion. The germ theory of disease had not yet been discovered and accepted, but trial and error and many suspicions were prevalent with thinking people. This discovery in itself would change the future of the world. America's first suspension bridge was built in 1796 by James Finley in Westmoreland, Pa.. In 1800 Henry Bell, a Scottish engineer, designed the first European steamship and Volta invented the electric battery. These technological breakthroughs would soon start an avalanche of world change.

Slavery in the New World had existed all across colonial America, the Caribbean and South America. Slavery also included vast numbers of white people under the euphemism of indentured servants. It died out in the North simply because it did not pay, and as the 18th century moved into the 19th century most people in the North and South alike thought it would very soon go out of existence everywhere because of the poor economics. But in 1793 a Yankee from New Haven, Connecticut, Eli Whitney, had invented the Cotton Gin. Then everything changed. When the constitution was ratified in 1789 it was not known that the growing of cotton could be made profitable in the southern states. The roller gin could clean only six pounds a day with slave labor. In 1784 eight bales of cotton were seized in Liverpool, England from an American ship on the grounds that so much cotton could not be the produce of the United States. It is significant to point out that at this time the big majority of the population in America was of English, Scottish or French descent. The massive migrations of Germans, Irish, and Italians with a substantial number of Chinese did not occur until the middle of the 19th century. It is also significant that slavery was outlawed in England at this time. With Whitney's new "saw gin", by which the cotton was pulled through parallel wires with openings too narrow for the seeds to pass, one slave could now clean 1,000 pounds of cotton per day! Now the short staple cotton which the southern states could grow so abundantly became the most profitable crop in America or for that matter anywhere. The world had developed an almost limitless appetite for cotton and the textile mills of England were the best in the world. In the deep South vast quantities of cotton could be raised cheaply with slave labor and the cotton gin. Slave labor was also looked upon as essential to this equation in order to realize the potential profits from this new bonanza of technology and agriculture. The exports of cotton leaped from 189,000 lbs. in 1791 to 21,000.000 lbs. in 1801 and doubled in three years. This represented about 7% of the nation's exports. By 1860 cotton made up about 57% of the nation's exports and the South had become a cotton empire. Nearly four million slaves were employed by then and slavery was viewed as an essential element for this southern prosperity.

To understand the slave problem accurately and its impact on urban settlements, its origins in America should be understood. Slavery has prevailed in all parts of human history for the last 10,000 years and probably before that time. This would include not only Europe and the Middle East, but also the Orient, Africa and with the American Indians, especially the Aztec and the Maya cultures.

Slavery was always an important part of warfare (to the victor go the spoils) and was the only source of energy for the public works and services needed by any culture trying to maintain or expand its religious or political realm. Slavery on the sea going galleys became common in the 15th century, with rowers instead of being free workers as in ancient times, became captives chained to their benches. This change was encouraged by the fact that great numbers of people were captured in the continuous wars and piratical raids of the Christian and Muslim powers around the Mediterranean against each other. The Turks, like the Romans, were given to slave raiding and slave owning on a huge scale; while during the Reformation the French and Spanish kings found the galleys a useful way to dispose of Protestants.

In the New World slavery became important because of sugar and the insatiable appetite of Europe for this financially attractive crop. Originally American Indians were impressed into this service, but they could not stand the regimentation required for the work and would perish either from the lash, European diseases or just the confinement. African blacks were soon found to have few of these shortcomings and were readily available from the black and white slave traders in Africa. Practically all of these slaves were employed in the islands of the Caribbean. Some of these were imported to Virginia and the Carolinas to cultivate tobacco and the little cotton that could be had before Whitney's cotton gin. This was in the 18th century. By the 19th century with the introduction of the cotton gin in 1793, this picture changed and slavery in the United States became part of big business.

Ironically, the same man, Eli Whitney, who introduced "King" cotton to the South, shortly afterwards introduced his next idea, the "Interchangeability of Parts" and the principle of "Mass Production". Although the idea of mass production was not new, no one had been able to make it work. In 1798, while

Thomas Jefferson was still thinking about the problems of mass production, Whitney entered into a contract with the United States Government to produce 10,000 muskets "in all parts precisely or as near as possible conformably to three patterns." There were many problems, but when Whitney designed a series of machine tools, especially his milling machine, which cut the desired parts from the metal stock to specified tolerances and then introduced the use of water power for production, the concept of mass production became a reality. The concept of tolerances and interchangeable parts was what made the system work. Eli Whitney was truly the father of mass production and with this new process the mill town or the factory town was born.

Up to this time all guns were hand made and for the most part all came from Europe, namely, England or France. If any part of the gun broke or had to be replaced, the new part had to be hand crafted and fitted to the broken gun. With mass production and the manufacturing of interchangeable parts, any broken part could be replaced and/or a new gun assembled from the manufactured parts in record breaking time.

By the turn of the century, 1800, America's population was 5.3 million including about 800,000 slaves. By 1806 the British cotton industry had 90,000 factory workers and 184,000 weavers. In 1807 Fulton launched the Clermont, a 150 foot steamboat that traveled 150 miles up the Hudson River in 32 hours. By 1815, just 22 years after Whitney's Cotton Engine, New England textile mills were processing 90,000 bales of cotton a year; up from only 500 bales in 1800. By 1822 cotton mills in Massachusetts were in production with water powered machinery. By 1826 one plant in Lowell turned out 2 million yards of cloth a year. Note, women were used in the labor force. In 1825 DeWitt Clinton's Erie Canal was completed connecting the Great Lakes with the Hudson River and the Atlantic Ocean and in 1826 an internal combustion engine was patented by Samuel Morse, a Connecticut inventor. In 1829 the first typographer, an early typewriter, was invented by a Mass. surveyor, William Burt. In 1832 Samuel Morse designed an improved electromagnetic telegraph. He did not apply for a patent until 1837. Cyrus H. McCormick, a Virginia inventor, patented the McCormick Reaper in 1834. The Reaper would revolutionize food production in the U.S. and the world. In that same year slavery was abolished in the British Empire.

In 1837 John Deere, a blacksmith, developed the first plow with a steel
mold board to plow the heavy sticky soil of the Midwest prairie. This invention
and the invention of Cyrus McCormick, the mechanical reaper, quickly
advanced mechanized agriculture and the industrial age in America.
McCormick set up a factory in Chicago in 1847 and began turning out machines
that made it easy to cover the western prairies with wheat. Even though
McCormick first introduced the reaper in Virginia, it was the North that took the
machine to its bosom and the production of wheat rose an astonishing 75% in
the 1850's and corn 40%. The South however eschewed the reaper and anything
else except cotton. Nothing could replace the King for them. Some reports
claimed that the city of Natchez, Miss., prior to 1860, had more millionaires
than any other city in the U.S.

Meanwhile this age of invention and discovery was gaining momentum. In
1844 the first telegraph message was sent from Washington D.C. to Baltimore,
"What hath God wrought?". In 1845 Erastus Bigelow, a Mass. inventor, started
building power looms for weaving carpets and other fabrics. In 1846 Elias
Howe patented a lock stitch sewing machine and in 1852 Elisha Otis designed a
passenger elevator. This invention would change the configuration of cities
forever. In 1857 Louis Pasteur, a French chemist and microbiologist, discovered
and formulated the "Germ Theory of Disease". This discovery would impact
world populations for years to come. By 1850 the population of the United
States was 23.1 million including 3.2 million slaves. Most of these inventions
and discoveries were in their infancy at this time, but the seeds of change were
well planted and waiting for practically anyone to harvest the bounty. In 1859
Charles Darwin published his "Origin of the Species" after his five years on the
Beagle collecting biological specimens from many parts of the world especially
the Galapagos Islands. This great insight into the evolution of life on earth
would change mankind's concept of life on earth for years to come.

By the middle of the 19th century the seeds of the industrial revolution had
taken firm root in the northern states. Even though the cultural make up of this
part of the country remained essentially rural, the massive immigrations from
Europe and the new inventions intensified the pressure on American cities for
urbanization. In spite of the war, from 1861 through 1865 more than 800,000
Europeans came to America, most of them from England, Ireland and Germany.
The McCormick reaper and combine, the new corn planter and the new steel

plow added so much mechanical muscle to the northern economy that Europe began to be concerned about the threat of American imports. As early as 1851 the McCormick reaper, the new Colt revolver and Goodyear rubber products were winning accolades at London's Crystal Palace Exhibition and by 1854 British manufacturers were complaining about U.S. imports.

Conversely the South eschewed any improvements by mechanized methods (except for the cotton gin) and chose instead to capitalize on the immediate profits resulting from "King Cotton" and the use of slave labor. This dichotomy soon resulted in a complete polarization of the country with one region moving ahead into the age of industrialization and the other region to an almost anachronistic view that life could remain the same without any change as long as "King Cotton" could retain his throne. This of course would be forever! By the late 1850's this polarization was reflected in the political views of the South and the Northern States. The South was content with making money by raising and shipping cotton with no interference of government regulations whatsoever. The North was moving with all deliberate speed into the industrial age taking advantage of its inventive ingenuity, the massive migrations of cheap labor from Europe, expanded rail transportation and its vast markets for the exportation of wheat. With the tools of mechanization, reaper, plow, etc., wheat was now big, big business. This combination of resources demanded more and more government regulation and protectionism for the North as opposed to the anathema for government by the South. The result was an ever increasing amount of pressure from the South to separate itself from Washington and any increase in government regulations. Notwithstanding the intractable issue of slavery, it was separation and secession which precipitated the war between the states.

No analysis of the evolution of American cities would be complete without an understanding of the impact of the Civil War on the American transition from a rural to an urban society. Although most historians record this war as the result of a fundamental difference in moral values, namely slavery, the evidence suggest that technology, or the absence of it, not moral turpitude was the more real and most basic cause which polarized the North against the South. After all the northern traders were the ones who procured the slaves from the African slavers for the South. Once this polarization was complete, only a final spark, a cause celebe, was needed to ignite the great conflict. The constitution did not specifically prohibit a state from secession, and still does not, so with such intensified feelings of alienation any southerner worth his salt could find strong moral and legal justification for his separation from the union if he or she believed that their economic survival depended on this separation.

Urban development has long been directly related to progress of technology. The Civil War was a driving force for the advancement of technology and the future of urban development. Many of the new technologies were still in the embryonic stage at the beginning of the war, but ensuing manpower shortages and a tremendous increase in demand for more production greatly accelerated technological development. As already mentioned, the Industrial Revolution was on a roll in the northern part of the U.S.. The South was almost reactionary in their refusal to adopt any improvements which were not immediately useful for the cotton industry. Railroads were mediocre to poor and practically no equipment or machinery was manufactured in the South and most importantly, cotton and tobacco were the only crops grown and the basis of the economy. Therefore except for the seaport towns all of the southern communities were small agricultural trading centers which provided only minimum services for the plantations and farms in the area. By contrast the urban centers in the North were undergoing very rapid growth with an increasing amount of immigration, growth of industries for iron and steel, manufacturing, textiles, and the development of a new wool industry which was soon to be a serious competitor to cotton.

With new standardized rail roads and a new locomotive industry, transportation was expanding at a rapid rate. Just before the war the locks and canal at Sault Sainte Marie, Michigan had been built and put into service. This opened up Lake Superior and an unlimited supply of iron ore to the mills in Pittsburgh which could now turn out cannon, railroad rails, iron plating for ships and locomotives. Pittsburgh had now rapidly become a mill town. Another most important development in agriculture was the expansion of the wheat crop. With the new equipment, the McCormick reaper, yields were increasing so fast that wheat was now an export commodity to England. Between 1861 and 1863 the North supplied Great Britain with 40% of its wheat and flour. The rail road and the rail head was now becoming the focal point for urban development in the North and western part of the U.S.. As food production increased on the farms and factories increased in the cities in the North with the new industries, the urban populations in the North increased compared to populations in the South which had minimal growth or remained static.

Under these circumstances it was only a matter of time before the break would come and declarations backed up by firm convictions for the right of secession would quickly lead to hostilities. In 1860 South Carolina seceded from the Union affirming the doctrine of States' Rights and in 1861 the bombardment of Fort Sumpter by the Confederates provided the spark that ignited the great war between the states. Had the logistics of the American Civil War made any kind of logical sense the response and results of all these events might have been entirely different. The facts however which we can see so clearly today reveal an almost ludicrous confrontation of opponents for such a conflict. Once the war was started its operations and in particular the tactics employed by the adversaries appear as sad epitaphs for those who fail to recognize change and the consequences of change. The gap between the two adversaries was well illustrated by a meeting on Christmas Eve, 1860 when William Tecumseh Sherman was speaking to a Southern friend on the futility of the threatening war. "The North can make a steam engine, locomotive or railway car; hardly a yard of cloth or a pair of shoes can you make. You are rushing into a war with one of the most powerful , ingeniously mechanical and determined people on earth-right at your doors. You are bound to fail."

From the onset the economical, political and technological position of the South was unrealistic and untenable. The basic strategy of the South was based on the belief that if the war became too expensive and wearisome for the North, the North would then abandon its altruistic and chauvinistic belief in the "Union Forever" and let the South separate with good riddance. There was considerable merit in this view since the profits of northern farmers had never been greater and there was little taste for the aggravation, expense and inconvenience of war. Lee and Davis structured practically all of their military movements and tactics around this strategy. An important part of the strategy was to get England to recognize the Confederacy as a separate country from the U.S.. As Lincoln encountered more and more difficulty continuing the war he turned the entire political situation around with the Emancipation Proclamation in 1862 which not only mobilized the morale and enmity of the North, but alienated the whole of Europe against the South with its slave culture. No one in Europe and in particular England could be allied with a country which openly encouraged and supported slavery. With this most basic setback in strategy the technological superiority of the North and the corresponding inferiority of the South came into sharp focus and the beginning of the end was in sight.

Most of the officer corps in both of the armies knew each other personally since they all went to the same school together at West Point, New York. All military tactics learned by each of the commands from the Point were based on the principles laid down by Napoleon in 1798-1812 who in turn developed his ideas based on the technology of his time and the resources he had available. Superimposing these tactics and ideas on the technology of 1862, '63, '64 and '65 resulted in one disaster after another for each of the battles fought in the war. Napoleon's tactics were developed around the use of the smoothbore cannon and musket with its limited range, short trajectory and extended time for reloading. The use of the rifled bore musket with its greater range, development of the Minie Ball, which reduced reloading time, the breech loading rifle with its cartridges and shorter time for reloading and of course the Spencer repeating rifle, made all such tactics obsolete. Unfortunately the commands for either side made no such adjustments in their tactics to accommodate the new technology and the resulting carnage for both of the armies provided grim testimony to this anachronistic thinking.

Except for some feeble attempts to employ such innovations as the submarine and the Spencer repeating rifle, the military almost completely sidestepped the advantages of the mechanical age. One exception to this policy was the development and use of steel clad ships for the navy. The battle of the Monitor and the Merrimac in 1862 revolutionized naval warfare. But other than this aberration basic military tactics and much of the strategy were based almost entirely on 18th century principles. The obsolete smooth bore musket with its practical range of 75 to 100 yards required a considerable effort to load the charge at the muzzle and prepare for firing of the weapon. At Gettysburg one musket was found that had been loaded 17 times without being fired once! Correspondingly, cavalry tactics were designed to take advantage of this extensive operation so that the enemy could be charged at full gallop during the time it took the soldier to reload his weapon. (This cavalry tactic even carried over into World War I and II.) Tactics for the infantry were also based on these principles and the corresponding drama for each encounter was to advance as far as one dared in order to encourage the enemy to "fire" first. If this challenge was successful, the enemy could then be "charged" with fully loaded weapons while he was engaged in the laborious task of reloading. The rifled barrel musket and the minie ball completely undermined this primitive tactic with its effective range of 300 to 400 yards which was more than double the range of the old smooth bore. The timing of the "charge" or the advance of the infantry therefore was completely upset with the range of this new rifle. But the tactics did not change accordingly! Battle after battle the infantry and the cavalry still waited and charged according to the old timetable and when those armies were encountered with the new weapons, the losses were devastating. One consequence was that the only really effective cavalry units for both North and South were the mounted rifle units who used the horses for speed and mobility and then dismounted and functioned as infantry regulars.

So it was with the smooth bore cannon and the use of canister and grapeshot which had very limited range. The rifled bore cannon with proximity and percussion fuses devastated the enemy whenever it was employed, but the officer corps did little to capitalize on this advantage because of inexperience and more importantly, the resistance to change. One of the biggest mistakes however, was the failure of the North to take advantage of the breechloading rifle or the famous Spencer repeating rifles. Had these new weapons been used by the North to their maximum advantage when they were available, (many officers and men bought their own.) the war might well have been shortened by 50% because of their vast increase in firepower and ease of deployment. One argument from the War Department was that a soldier couldn't carry that much ammunition. There was also a strong prejudice among officers against all arms loading at the breech. This prejudice which had prevailed for many years, was accompanied by a strong desire to protect the investment of several million dollars in the old muskets from the revolutionary war which were still in the armories. The muzzle loading musket of the American Revolution, with a percussion lock in place of the older flint lock, was the standard infantry arm. It remained so even to the end of the Civil War, although breechloaders had for some time been proved successful and repeaters, such as the Spencer, were available in 1861. Confederate General E.P. Alexander is quoted as saying that, "had the Federal infantry been armed from the first with even the breechloaders available in 1861, the war would have been terminated within a year."

Along with this obsolete thinking there was also a great deal of ignorance of the impact of new technology on basic military logistics. The railroads in the North were almost overbuilt before the war. Vast quantities of wheat and corn were moved by rail throughout the North including the Midwest and even parts of the west. By contrast the rail systems of the South were so poor and obsolete, they could not even be used by government officials for commuting much less for the movement of troops or war material. The North used this resource with maximum effectiveness. The rails moved troops and supplies from one front to another with a speed and effectiveness never seen before in the history of warfare. Lee was completely confounded with these movements. Grant's move from Vicksburgh to Virginia was unbelievable to the southern forces. Yet this rapid and unprecedented move was one of the most decisive factors in Lee's surrender at Appomattox. Along with this great advantage in transportation the North also used the telegraph to unprecedented advantage. At the start of the war in 1861 telegraph wires were completely strung between New York and San Francisco providing instant communications across the continent. Of equal importance to military operations, this instant communication was a quantum leap forward for industry and commerce. Everything from news reporting to bills of lading and inventory control were transmitted by the telegraph. Of special importance, practically every town in America was in the communications network provided by the telegraph.

Notwithstanding the many advantages of these technological improvements, great numbers of the military corps held on to atavistic principles, techniques and equipment much to the detriment and extension of the war. The most classic anachronism that prevails even to this day is the bayonet. Although an excellent tool for opening tin cans, used as a spit for roasting an occasional rabbit or cutting fire wood, only one victim was officially recorded as killed by a bayonet in the battle of Shilo in the Civil War. Out of 7, 302 wounded during part of Grant's wilderness campaign, only six were listed as being injured by sword or bayonet. The 10-barrel Gatling Gun, a machine gun that fired 250 rounds per minute, was patented in 1862, but never saw action in the war. This tremendous increase in fire power could have changed the course of the war.

The technology accelerated by the war also introduced many domestic and commercial changes which prevail to this day. With the improvement in manufacturing mass production and especially food processing, Gilbert C. Van

Camp of pork and beans fame made his fortune during the Civil War. Gail Borden in 1861 contracted to sell condensed milk in a can to the soldiers and Herr Schrafft suddenly prospered by turning out gumdrops which the home folks sent to the troops. As you might expect Henry Du Pont prospered very well with his gunpowder sales from 1861 forward. Richard Gatling also did well although his rapid fire gun was not used in the war.

The war finally came to an end not so much from any great feats of generalship or major military victories, although there were certainly examples of each for both sides, but rather from the fact that both sides were very weary and the South became exhausted after their meager resources were spent and could not be replaced. Were there other reasons for the South losing the war? Yes indeed, but aside from the fact that the South had eschewed new technology in favor of King Cotton, the reasons are varied and controversial to say the least. When the war started Lincoln attempted to treat it as an insurrection which he expected to put down with relatively little effort. This soon proved to be an illusion. The success of the Confederate military offensives in 1862 finally convinced Lincoln and the Republicans that they must mobilize everything and destroy all Southern resources used to sustain the Confederate war effort. The most important resource was the Southern labor force which was mostly slaves. When congress confiscated the property of the Confederates which included slaves and Lincoln issued the Emancipation Proclamation in 1862 to free the slaves, the blow to the South was irreparable. Along with this move Great Britain made known that they could not recognize the Confederacy since it was a slave state.

In addition, the English mills discovered Egyptian cotton less expensive than running the northern blockade. From this moment forward especially with the victories of Grant at Vicksburg and Mead at Gettysburg in 1863, the fate of the South was sealed.

The South continued the war because of their belief that the North would grow weary of the war and abandon the effort to hold the union together. The strategy of winning a war with inferior resources was not new. The classic case was the American revolution which pitted inferior forces against a vastly superior power. The British army was the best in the world at the time and of course the case of the U.S. in Vietnam in recent times is another example of how victory does not always go to the biggest army if it becomes too expensive.

Perhaps too much of the Confederate strategy rested on this belief in spite of their very weak position at the beginning of the war and their very poor technological base.

What the war did however, was to accelerate the industrialization of America. Industries and to a considerable extent Commerce were very small and fragmented before the war. The war created manpower shortages and increased demand for just about everything. New machines were employed in agriculture and manufacturing which increased production and of course increased the size of the cities and towns and the classic mill town came into its own at this time.

In retrospect we now see how this horrible disaster resulted from an enormous ignorance of the impact of modern (1861-65) technology on the social, economic and especially the military operations for the country. This appears to be true not only for the war itself, but also for the sequence of events that led up to the war. If anything could be learned from this war it might be the lesson of ignorance pitted against the inexorable changes of technology. Unfortunately, the aftermath of the war proved that no such lesson was learned, Technology continued to forged ahead at an unprecedented rate, but the trends were again ignored and the seeds of future conflicts were planted in America and Europe as well.

CHAPTER 5

WESTERN MIGRATIONS AND NEW TOWNS IN THE 19TH CENTURY

The conclusion of the Civil War set the stage for the country to enter the 20th Century. After the dreadful tragedy of Lincoln's assassination, the government stumbled and then bumbled the recovery with what amounted to a do-nothing policy for the reconstruction of the South. Lincoln's idea of compensating the southern slave holders for their loss of slave power was met with scorn and buried in the ignorant and maudlin polemics of Congress and the military. In this kind of vacuum and with the severe damages that had been delivered, healthy reconstruction and growth in the South was painfully slow. The country now directed its attention westward. The West was a vast area of mystery and suspicion for most Americans. From the Mississippi to the Rocky Mountains was thought of as one enormous uncharted desert. The movement to the West started not with any organized plan of action, but rather as a fortuitous combination of political neglect, technological improvements and perhaps most importantly, the beginning of a new and different philosophy for the control of an individual's destiny in a strange, hostile land.

This new philosophy developed as a result of the work of Charles Darwin. This new idealistic pragmatism shook the very foundations of established thought throughout the intellectual world. When Darwin postulated his theory of the Origin of the Species in 1859, the effect on the modern world was comparable to the effect of Homer's Tales on the ancient world of the Greeks. As Ulysses demonstrated to his world that man could not only cope with the gods, but in some cases even control them, so Darwin's theory revealed to the modern world that the forces of nature followed a "predictable" pattern of development, albeit over protracted periods of geologic time. The world was not static and immutable. On the contrary, the world was in constant state of change! Since change was not only an important part of the process of life, but perhaps more importantly, the result of "Variation and Natural Selection", men who could survive the new environment would prevail and be successful. Correspondingly, men were not predestined to live the life of their fathers in a pattern set by Providence. Instead men were free to reach out, explore, succeed or fail as part of the very process itself! It would appear that this new point of view had a profound affect on the rate of technological change. The period from 1850 to 1950 witnessed the greatest number of technological changes and improvements in the history of mankind.

In 1867 Alfred Nobel invented dynamite and the era of smokeless powder began along with this indispensable tool for the construction of our roads, bridges, canals, factories and houses. In 1868 the first practical typewriter was invented and in 1869 the first transcontinental railroad was completed linking the Atlantic and Pacific oceans. The frontier had now moved off of the eastern seaboard U.S. and the towns and cities were now taking root at the railheads, river crossings, ports of America and wherever the railroad thought there was a market for freight. In 1874, Joe Glidden of New Hampshire invented the first practical barbed wire for fencing. This would have an immediate and forceful impact on the settlement of the West and Midwest. In 1876, Alexander Graham Bell invented the telephone which with the telegraph opened up the age of telecommunication in America and the world. Tom Edison in 1879 invented the first practical electric light which would soon replace the gas lamps in our cities and eventually all of the oil lamps in our homes to illuminate our lives for the 20th century. In that same year George B. Selden, an engineer, developed a three cylinder internal combustion engine and used it to power a "horseless carriage". In France, De Lesseps started the Panama Canal Company to build a canal through the Isthmus of Panama. (In 1887 the famous French engineer Alexandre Gustave Eiffel was engaged to design the famous locks for the canal.)

Other technological events had helped set the stage for the development of the West and the evolution of our cities. Of fundamental importance for the westward movement was the U.S. Public Lands Survey Act instituted by the

Ordinance of May 20, 1785, by the Continental Congress. The rectangular system of square mile sections, townships and counties appears amazingly simple in concept, but even though it had been applied in Europe to some extent, its application to American territories West of the Alleganies proved to be almost revolutionary in the way it shaped the development of American farms and cities. Largely inspired by Thomas Jefferson, the grid system represented a new relationship between people and the land. With most of the Indian wars over and expansion of the early colonial towns limited, the people no longer saw the need for living in compact defensible settlements and the practice of living in the village and working in the fields some miles away became more and more impractical. In addition, thousands of immigrants were arriving from Europe. The Scots, the Irish, the Germans and the Welsh who had no liking for those closely knit communities where everyone was fixed to a prescribed neighborhood and had to support the established church. They wanted no part of the old system. The yearning was for privacy and freedom, and the western lands of America offered the opportunity for these goals. The new survey system quickly became the convenient instrument for achieving this goal for millions of Americans then and ever since. Jefferson's original thinking was that each of the Townships made up of 36 one mile square sections, would become a community center thus fostering thousands of enclaves of democracy. Section 16 therefore was allocated for the construction of a school which was to become the nucleus of the community. As we now know this did not happen. Notwithstanding the enormous amount of hard labor required of farming, the independent and isolated farm was the epitome of independence. That was the goal that people strived for. The grid system established by the Public Land Survey Act set the pattern for this development and for the most part that's the way it did happen. This same grid system also set the pattern or the location of the county seat of government, the road system and in many cases the rail heads. A theory was that the county seat should be no more than one days travel from the farm using a team and wagon.

During this same period the railroad moved West with all deliberate speed. The road followed the line of least resistance and the most economical cost of construction. The goal was to capture the huge agricultural markets in the new

West and move these products East. The art of bridge building at this time evolved into a science which accompanied the great advances in the technology of making steel and building foundations. This resulted in a network of transportation across the country that had not been seen since the Roman Empire built its system of roads throughout Europe. The invention of the telegraph brought "instant" communication from its lines on the railroad right-of-ways to the market centers in the East.

One of the most interesting innovations that occurred at this time was the invention of barbed wire. Fences are an absolute requirement not only for the practice of agriculture, but as a practical matter for the ownership of land. Up to this time fences were made for the most part from local materials and were very expensive in time and money. Split rails, stones, brush or bramble and ditches were the most common. Just maintaining rail fences absorbed about one-twelfth of the total annual labor on a farm. For the country as a whole in the 1860s, the cost of fencing for crop agriculture ran twice the value of the land! In the western prairies where there were no trees and the farming nesters encountered the cattle ranchers who were using the public lands for grazing, the lack of good fencing presented serious problems. The introduction of good and economical barbed wire fencing solved this problem, but not without considerable difficulties in reconciling the two uses of the same land and water for farming and raising cattle.

The American diaspora that emerged from the eastern seaboard on to the western prairies was motivated by the spirit of independence and the hope of making a profit, but technology was the engine that drove the movement and created the America we know today. In this very short period the railroads, telegraph, steel bridges, barbed wire, the reaper, the planter and the combine all were introduced to the agricultural economy with spectacular results. Many new towns were created at the railroad and river crossings and the resulting increases in food production now permitted the cities to expand and increase their populations to meet the new demands for manufacturing. Now as the population densities of the towns and cities increased, problems increased too. Most significantly were the disease problems which were aggravated by the ignorance of their cause and etiology. Morbidity and mortality rates increased as the cities increased in size.

In 1864 a discovery was made in southern France that not only changed the design and operation of cities, but changed the history of civilization itself. Louis Pasteur (1822-1895) a chemist and microbiologist (the first one!) declared with certainty that minute organisms causing fermentation were not "spontaneously generated". The Germ Theory of Disease was born. The medical community was reluctant to accept this theory, but in 1881 a public test on anthrax proved the theory to be valid. It would be many years however, before the public would accept this concept and even today some people don't accept it. Today it is difficult to imagine any aspect of life without the understanding of this fundamental concept. The history of the medical corps of the Union and Confederate armies offers some idea of operations without the knowledge of this theory. Of the estimated 750,000 deaths in this conflict, as many as one half have been estimated to have been caused by tetanus alone! These were practically all in the eastern theater where the wounded were hospitalized in barns where horses had been quartered for many years. On the western fronts the unsettled territories had not yet time to develop the dreaded organisms. Surgeons wiped their knives clean on their aprons to be ready for the next patient and nurses rinsed the sponges so they could be reused. The concept of sterilization never occurred to anyone. Mosquitoes and flies were considered pest, but the idea that they might carry disease was unheard of. And this was just a little over one hundred years ago!

The Germ Theory of Disease is now accepted over most of the civilized world, but the older cities have not completely changed to accommodate all of the conditions embraced by the theory. It can be said without equivocation that no other factor influences the design, construction and operation of a city more than the Germ Theory of Disease. Ever since ancient times sewers were built to prevent flooding and remove the storm water. With the introduction of the new germ theory of disease and the invention of the flush water toilet in the latter part of the century, the storm sewers in the cities were now used to accept the sanitary waste as well as the storm water. While one problem appeared to be solved, a more serious problem resulted from the concentration of the sanitary waste in the rivers and lakes which in so many cases also provided the drinking water for the towns. The problem of contaminating the water supplies was exacerbated with the growth of manufacturing which also discharged its industrial waste into the public sewers and thence the public water supply. Soon elaborate and expensive waste treatment facilities were being installed at the most serious problem locations, but in too many instances the concentration of the waste was too great for even the most sophisticated treatment facilities. The problems of too many people in too small a space began to grow in earnest.

No period in the history of civilization had ever witnessed such an avalanche of technological and/or scientific discovery as the 19th century. With the generous donations of free land to the railroads by the U.S. Government, 20,000 miles of track were laid in ten years! Telegraph lines were strung from city to city and every rail stop in between across the whole continent. Cables were laid across the Atlantic and in 1876 the telephone added lightening communication to the American scene. The labor mix was changing in this post civil war period so that the number of farm workers needed to operate the farms and "feed" the cities decreased drastically. In the decade from 1860 to 1870 the total number of manufacturing establishments increased by 80% and the value of manufactured products by 100%. Portland cement came on the market in the 1870's which along with Nobel's invention of dynamite enabled the construction industry to advance to heights it had never known. The development of the internal combustion engine by Otto Benz along with the development of the petroleum industry in Europe and America brought the first automobiles to American roads before the turn of the century. The Hoe rotary press and the electrotype process worked a revolution in the printing of newspapers and books. In 1883 the Brooklyn Bridge was completed utilizing Robeling's invention of steel rope and the first pneumatic caissons for major structural foundations. This new advancement in bridge building opened up entirely new possibilities for the future of transportation and especially for the evolution of cities. The application and development of all of these improvements did not occur at a uniform rate throughout the country. The use of electric power was severely limited by the short distance that direct current could be transmitted from its generator source. It was the discovery of the use of alternating current in Europe for the transmission of electric power along with the first "successful" incandescent electric light by Thomas Edison that provided the impetus and momentum to expand the use of electric power in industry and homes at all of the urban centers in the country.

Europe's demands for American cotton, wheat and pork could not be satisfied. In the fifty years after Appomattox the U.S. ran up a cumulative favorable balance of trade of more than 2 1/4 billion dollars, and by 1910 annual exports had passed the $2 billion mark. Labor supply was cheap and plentiful. From the farms and country villages, from the ranks of women and children and from the teaming cities of Italy, Austria, Germany and Poland millions of workers poured into the industrial centers of America. In the thirty years after 1870 the total number of wage earners increased from twelve to twenty nine million, and for those engaged in manufacturing from less than three to seven million over the same period. The impact on the cities was profound. The cities were ill prepared to accept these massive population movements to their industrial centers. Unlike the earlier waves of immigrants who yearned for land, privacy and independence, this new group moved for jobs and freedom from the tyranny of poverty and/or politics. It should be noted that the very "freedom" which encouraged the great industrial expansion in these urban centers, militated against rigid zoning laws, building codes and regulations of any kind! The results of this combination were shameful to say the least. The railroad apartments of New York City, the row housing of Chicago, Pittsburgh, Cleveland and Detroit resulted in population densities totally incompatible with public health facilities and standards. Water Supplies for consumption and fire protection, sewage treatment plants, trash collections and disposal along with social services, e.g. police protection, education, hospitals, etc. were just ignored for years setting the stage for the pollution problems of the mid 20th century. Note: New York City and Detroit still discharge raw sanitary sewage into the Hudson and Detroit rivers with their combined sewer collection systems notwithstanding federal and state laws to the contrary.

There was a common rationale for the movement and growth of industries in the major urban centers. Manufacturing industries had to have power (either electric or steam), rail transportation, labor supply, water supplies and sewerage

services. With few exceptions these were all available in the cities East of the
Mississippi. Other ancillary services were also needed. Telephone and
telegraph, banking, coal and/or oil storage facilities and construction services to
build the plants and offices for the operations. Labor of course had to have
housing and transportation such as street cars, buses or subways. Grocery stores,
schools, churches and municipal services, e.g. police, fire department, water
supplies and sewer service, etc. All of this was available or made available so
industry could thrive in the city. Manufacturing had now risen to equal status
with Shipping and Agriculture as the main economic base to support the large
cities. What shaped the configuration of these cities were the technological
forces that shaped the industries. These same forces also shaped the people.

It's important to understand how the industrial revolution shaped the cities
and towns of America. A city must have an economic base to sustain itself or it
cannot survive. It is inadequate to say that if a city has a fine entertainment
center or nice cultural attractions that it can remain viable and continue to grow
and prosper. What is essential for economic health is that function or activity in
the city that brings money into the city from outside of the city. This is the
money that meets payrolls, pays the taxes, supports the restaurants, shopping
centers, libraries, social services, churches, schools, zoos, cultural centers,
museums, police departments, fire departments, builds the waste treatment
plants, water supplies and bridges. If the economic base becomes so weak or is
lost altogether then none of these facilities or services can survive without an
outside subsidy. The city then becomes a parasite or dies and then reverts to its
original state of farmland, forest, or green meadow. This latter fate has
happened to many cities throughout history all over the world.

When America moved West early in the 19th century, Agriculture was the
primary economic base that supported the individual farms and the small farm
towns that still dot much of the countryside. These were small trading centers
located for the most part along the rivers, lakes, canals and coast lines of the
eastern United States. Most of these small towns were trading centers for all of
the things needed on the farm, but could not be produced on the farm. The
lumber mill, the flour mill, the blacksmith, dry goods, medicines, etc. along with
the church, the school, the hotel and the saloon were the usual facilities and

services making up the towns along the Mississippi, the Ohio, the Hudson, the Potomac, the Delaware, the Tennessee, the Savanna and hundreds of smaller and less well known rivers in the eastern part of the country. But it was the new technologies that made many of these towns the major urban centers that they became in the later part of the century. Boston became the shoe capital of the country. Massachusetts and Connecticut with their many small towns became the center of the machine-tool industry in America. Pittsburgh, a town of major military importance in the 18th century, became the capital of the country for making steel. Detroit at this time was the stove capital of the country. The virgin white pines of northern Michigan soon made Bay City, Michigan on Lake Huron, the lumber center for the country. Grand Rapids, Michigan became the furniture capital of the country. Akron, Ohio became the center of the rubber industry and Canton, Ohio was producing the largest steel presses in the world. New York City already endowed with excellent harbors and the major port of entry into the United States soon added textile mills, printing presses and with the advent of the telegraph and the telephone, it became the banking and trading capital for America and later the world. Seattle, Washington with its magnificent harbors and warm water port that serviced the northwest and Alaska, soon added the canning industry and lumber industry to its strong economic base. Chicago became the meat packing capital for the country and the world. Chicago soon became one of the busiest railroad centers in the world. McCormick started the manufacture of his famous McCormick Reaper in Chicago in 1848. This company soon became the International Harvester Co., one of the largest producers of agricultural implements in the world. Many other manufacturing companies soon started in Chicago and not long after the canal was opened in Sault St. Marie, Michigan in 1850, allowing the iron ore to be shipped from northern Michigan and Minnesota, to the steel mills in Chicago and Gary, Indiana soon rivaled Pittsburgh for the amount of tonnage produced. Chicago was on its way to becoming one of the largest urban centers in the world. The Erie Canal which opened up the Great Lakes to the Atlantic Ocean launched the city of Cleveland, Ohio as a major urban center and the city grew to greater heights with the completion of the canal which connected Lake Erie to the Ohio River. This major transportation hub continued to expand with the

movement of lumber, copper, iron ore and chemicals all shipped on the great
lakes freighters and schooners which moved the materials from the mines and
mills to the center of the country. Most of the sailing vessels were gone by the
end of the century, all replaced by steam.

In all of these locations as well as many others, the economic base was a
particular manufacturing industry, mining operation or strategic transportation
location. What created and continued to nourish these urban centers was the
new continuously improved technology that produced what was needed or in
demand in the country or in the world. Some of the great hallmarks of history
have been the result of ideas that inspired men and nations to move for good or
ill, but without the technology, much of what we know of as history would
never have happened. Indeed, the technology not only enabled the historic
events to take place, but in many cases it was the technology that was the
movement!

Historians have traditionally been reluctant, if not downright resistant, to
recognize the technological achievements of the times and in particular how
these accomplishments have been the prime movers of our history and created
the world we know today. And of course the men and women who provided us
with these improvements in our lives have for too long been hidden in the
shadows of our history books. If we have learned anything up to this time it
should be that "Function Follows Form," or expressed another way, our life
style today is the result of our technology.

If there ever could be a classic illustration of technology shaping the lives of
people and in particular the urban centers in America, it would be the way the
railroads developed and colonized the land from the Mississippi to the Rockies
in the middle of the 19th century. In this vast region of unsettled land the
railroads laid the track, established the towns and then recruited the settlers to
populate them. The railroad decided where the towns would be, the name of the
town and what the town would look like. Although rivers, canals and sea ports
had been the principal location of cities and towns in the eastern part of the
country, the western part of the country was not so well endowed. Most of the
waterways West of the Mississippi were too shallow for navigation and there
were not many rivers to begin with. The Platte River is alleged to be a mile wide

and one inch deep! Congress, seeking to encourage settlement in the West, gave the railroads enormous grants of land between 1850 and 1870 in areas that later became some of the richest farming country in the world. In the same period, a wave of immigration along with the Homestead Act of 1862 brought many farmers to the region.

The railroad companies in Chicago, St. Paul or St. Louis planned their lines according to the amount of freight they thought each region would generate. The towns were spaced at regular intervals to secure all of the trade from the farmers in the immediate area. If the towns were too far apart, a competing rail line could capture the traffic by building its own town nearby, if they were too close together, they would take each others business. In general the towns were about six miles apart (the width or depth of a Township), but this could vary based on the type of farming in the region. Regions made up of dairy farms could place their towns closer together because the farms were relatively small, but those towns in the open rangeland of the West in the beef cattle county were farther apart. Although these towns were not the same as the "company" towns of the mining, steel making or textile towns of the East, they shared some of the same problems, namely the owners were located hundreds of miles away. Those towns located at the intersection of two competing rail lines often grew into large cities.

Railroad towns looked different too. The companies used a limited set of town plans along their lines and one company's plans looked very much like any other. Old fashioned river towns in the East had spread out along the banks of the rivers and then expanded outward as they grew since river-front property was more valuable. Railroad towns by contrast, were centered around a single main street, usually at right angles to the tracks (this was called the Tee-town), because rail-front property was only valuable to grain elevators and the railroad itself. The rail line was usually at one end of town, with most of the development occurring away from it. This reduced the accident rate by reducing the need to cross the tracks. It also created an area beyond the station and the rail line called "the other side of the tracks." These unincorporated areas attracted drifters, tramps, migrant workers and others the locals found to be undesirable.

Names of the towns were a unique feature of the railroad. The names were "off the wall" in many cases. When the Missouri Pacific built its line through Kansas in the 1880s, it named fourteen towns after members of the champion St. Louis Browns baseball team. Street names were just as arbitrary. One plat used by several railroads was patterned on Philadelphia, with a square central park. Towns built on this plan even used the same street names as the original Philadelphia. Names and designs were not the only things the railroad controlled. Because they owned much of the surrounding land, they could decide who would be allowed to open stores in a new town. The companies had a clear idea of what type of people they wanted and where they wanted them placed. They believed that native born white Americans and immigrants from Britain were best suited to run businesses, while German, Scandinavian and certain Eastern European immigrants would make better farmers. Southern Europeans were thought of primarily as laborers who belonged in the mines and the factories.

One of the most interesting results of the railroad movement West in Canada and the United States, and certainly one of the most essential parts of our contemporary life style, was the standardization of time. If ever there was a question about the impact of technology on our life style and the way a person views their position in the general scheme of things, the concept of time and the standardization of time must rank high for such influence. The contemporary view is that time is an entity, something very real to be conserved, saved, quantified, measured and even as a fourth dimension. Time flies, heals, waits for no man; time is money, time is of the essence! In fact, time as an entity does not even exist. All time is a function of velocity and distance. It (time) is a function of these two variables, but as a practical matter it is very important to be able to measure time so you know when to plant seed, harvest crops, collect taxes, look for game to return to pasture, determine when the river will rise to flood stage, put the potatoes on for dinner or leave for vacation.

Thus calendars and time pieces have been devised to measure these important events. Some of these calendars go back thousands of years, ever since the agricultural revolution. These calendars and some ingenious time pieces to measure the time of day or night at a particular location did a magnificent job for a long time. Chinese water clocks and sand glasses were among the first mechanical clocks and incidentally still do a good job for many occasions. In 1581 Galileo discovered that the duration of a pendulum's swing is independent of the scope of its swing and ever since the pendulum clock has been worked well all over the world. All of these calendars and time pieces did an excellent job for telling the time at the place you were at. Your time was always correct at your location on the surface of the earth. When the sun reached its zenith in the daytime sky, it was 12:00 noon. It would take 24 hours for the sun to make its complete circuit to 12:00 noon the next day, etc. The system served well in the 19th century and even as late as 1870 Britain and France each had their own time zones. Greenwich time for England and Paris time for France. And even in America telling time was not a problem until the movement West and the coming of the railroad. Then the United States and Canada were in deep trouble. Between 1870 and 1880 confusion was king. The problem was exacerbated with the telegraph which was used to schedule departures, loadings, arrivals, ticket sales and of course which trains were going to be using which track at a particular time. Finally, Mr. Sanford Fleming of Canada, and Mr. Charles Dowd of the United States put forth a system of 24 standard meridians, each 15 degrees apart. These meridians are the center of 24 time zones; in each zone the time adopted would be uniform and it would change one hour in passing from one time zone to the next.

We now take standard time zones for granted in our everyday life, but the fact is that our economy, social fabric and even our military and political life would collapse without the use of standard time and for this standard we are indebted to the railroad.

Indeed, the Iron Horse had created the towns of the country side and to a considerable extent, altered the lives of the people in those towns as well as the many other towns and cities of America.

PART II

URBANIZATION IN THE 20TH CENTURY

CHAPTER 6

CITIES OF THE 20TH CENTURY AND WORLD WARS

C ities and towns of the 19th century in the United States entered the 20th century with almost euphoric optimism. The gas lights and gilded carriages of the gay 90's carried over to the turn of the century with the enthusiasm of Theodore Roosevelt's push for growth and expansion. When congress passed the Spooner Act in 1902 authorizing the financing and building of the Panama Canal, Roosevelt followed in 1903 with naval warships to Panama to support the Panama separatist against Columbia. In that same year the U.S. and Panama signed a treaty which gave the U.S. a ten mile strip of land across Panama and the completion of the Panama Canal was started by the United States. Yellow fever had defeated the French attempt to complete the canal, but in 1903 when William Gorgas, a U.S. army surgeon, controlled an epidemic in Havana, Cuba by killing mosquitoes and destroying the breeding areas, this problem was identified and solved. Such grand projects spread the optimism over the whole country. Cities and towns were still small by today's standards, but social problems were beginning to reach alarming proportions in the larger cities as new immigrants continued to pour into the country. The smaller towns remained to a considerable extent the same self sufficient communities they had been. Furniture came from the local cabinet maker, shoes from the shoemaker, meat from the butcher shop, carriages and harness from the local carriage maker, etc. However, as the new century got underway changes in the small town began to appear. The mill town became more conspicuous with the new steel mills which were now conglomerates, and the textile mills along with the mines now sponsored their own company towns. The electric motor had been added to the sewing machine in 1886.

Public health was still a big problem at the turn of the century. Infectious diseases including Yellow Fever, Tuberculosis, Typhoid and Pneumonia were the big killers, but it must be remembered that the germ theory of disease was still not completely accepted and sanitary engineering was primitive to say the least.

As the 19th century moved into the 20th century technology was on a roll and it seemed like it would never stop. One discovery or invention seemed to usher in the next technological advancement. Many of these inventions also changed fashions. They all changed our life style. As Winston Churchill is said to have pointed out; We fashion the machines and then the machines fashion us. In 1901 Willis Carrier invented the forerunner of the air conditioner which he patented in 1911 and in that same year King Gillette started to manufacture the modern safety razor with disposable blades. Within a few years ladies hemlines began to rise and men's beards slipped out of fashion. Shortly after the turn of the century the first successful heavier than air machine that could fly was introduced at Kitty Hawk, North Carolina in 1903. Orville and Wilbur Wright flew this motorized airplane 852 feet in a flight that lasted 59 seconds. In that same year a Packard automobile crossed the United States in 52 days driving from San Francisco to New York and by 1905 there were 77,988 registered automobiles in the United States. Most significantly, as the cities in America began to grow and multiply, the most damaging earthquake in the history of the country destroyed the central part of San Francisco. Most of the damage was from the fires that followed the severe quake. It was noteworthy that practically no one had earthquake insurance, but almost everyone had fire insurance. In 1907 George W. Goethals of the Army Corps of Engineers was appointed to direct the construction of the Panama Canal and in 1908 Henry Ford introduced his Model T, which cost $850. By 1909 his company was turning out 19,000 cars a year. Ford applied Eli Whitney's discovery of interchangeable parts and mass production to the assembly of automobiles and by 1926 the price had dropped to $310. By 1910 the population of the U.S. was 92 million. Almost 9 million of these were immigrants who had arrived since 1900. The electric washing machine was introduced and where ever electricity was available, it was quickly adopted. The drudgery of the wash board and the hand wringer still prevailed on the farm which was most of the nation since electricity would not reach the farm until the great depression of the 1930s.

One of the difficulties of these times was that people could not thoroughly comprehend the significance of these events which were happening at an increasing rate of speed. Along with all of the new inventions and discoveries came entire new technologies for weapons. In 1911 John M. Browning, a Utah gunsmith, invented the Browning automatic pistol. This was quickly followed by the water cooled machine gun and the British Lewis machine gun which was mounted on airplanes. Airplanes and dirigibles as well as submarines added a third dimension to warfare that was never anticipated by the military strategist in planning for the next war. These new weapons along with the tremendous increase in production capability soon added to the armies of Europe destructive power that even they did not realize. Reckless demands were then made on one country by another when the Austrian Archduke Ferdinand and his wife were assassinated by Serbian nationalist in Sarajevo in 1914. Practically all of the ruling families of these countries were related either by blood or marriage and they were constantly quarrelling with each other, but none of them understood the forces they were dealing with. The great war in Europe overshadowed one of the most significant technological achievements in history. The Panama Canal was completed in 1914. It was 40 miles long from the Atlantic to the Pacific and cost about $365 million. This would impact the economies of the United States and the World for years to come. Shortly after, in 1915, The Ford plant produced its one millionth automobile in Michigan.

When the participating countries started into this conflict they had a fairly conventional viewpoint of war that was rooted in the systems and practices of the late 18th and 19th century. The professional armies would engage in battle and very often the mass of the people would watch the struggle from the sidelines. The American Civil War had demolished much of this myth, but the rest of the world had not learned from this experience. More importantly perhaps, no one in history had ever mobilized such massive armies before with such powerful weapons. Modern technology had brought the art of weapons design and production to a stage never before achieved and the arsenals of the belligerents could scarcely hold the munitions and the weapons for the armies.

In 1917 America joined the allies in the war against the central powers and in 1918 Browning invented the Browning Automatic Rifle (BAR).

The old military tradition which prevailed for thousands of years, idealized combat as a contest between equally armed warriors. Women and children were not involved although the victor might take them as prizes. What was important in these contest was strength and bravery, not the weapons. In fact some of the warriors from Homer's stories would not use the bow for they could not fight their enemies by standing far away from them. By the start of W.W.I this point of view had turned around by 180 degrees. The rifle, machine gun, artillery shell and the aerial bomb now dominated the battlefield and not only killed the enemy soldier, but killed the women, children and obliterated the towns and cities! Observers of the battle of Ravenna in 1512, first battle decided by an artillery barrage, considered it mass destruction when one cannon ball claimed 33 casualties. A year later, at Novara, also in Italy, cannon killed 700 in three minutes. Then in 1803 Henry Shrapnel developed the first exploding artillery shell which contained smaller projectiles. This development made "mass destruction" routine. When W.W.I finally ended the casualty list was staggering. For all of the belligerents including the U.S. there were over 37 million military casualties including 8.54 million killed. Civilian casualties were not counted, but entire towns and villages along with their populations were wiped off the face of the earth. Indeed the Ends always justified the Means and little or no thought was ever given to the civilian populations.

Other than the military casualties of 350,000 of which 126,000 died, the U.S. did not suffer as did France, Russia or Great Britain from the great war. American had 4,355,000 men mobilized. No battles took place on American soil and naval action was almost non existent in American waters. Except for those who lost a loved one in the war, most Americans prospered and made substantial gains. A major exception to this generalization was the terrible influenza epidemic which had traveled West from Europe to the U.S. and then spread to 46 states. Before it ended in 1919 about 500,000 people died. Throughout the world at least 20 million people died and over a billion were ill from this modern plague. Urban congestion was a major factor. Few lessons, if any, seemed to have been learned from W.W. I, but shortly afterwards the cities, especially in America, took on a new configuration. The growth of the manufacturing industries in the urban centers continued at an unprecedented rate. What before had been fledgling crafts and works of craftsmanship now became major industries and the public couldn't buy enough of their products. The automobile, the washing machine, sewing machines, pharmaceutical, books, newspapers, magazines, radios and by the late 20s, refrigerators, prepackaged foods and canned foods. In addition, a new transportation system using passenger airplanes became familiar parts of the American lexicon. With the basic production facilities for all of these technological products located in the urban centers, most of their supporting industries also located there to control their cost and improve their service. The housing for labor, industrial suppliers, banking centers, the retail merchants, the schools, hospitals, theatres, rail road stations, hotels, office buildings, and of course all of the municipal services were in the urban centers. In this same period a new machine introduced by the Otis brothers in 1889, changed the configuration and life style of the cities more than any other machine in the previous thousand years. It was the electric elevator installed in New York City! In 1901 an electric escalator was installed in Gimbals Department Store in Philadelphia. The explosive growth of the cities now expanded vertically! By 1930 practically every commercial, institutional, industrial and multi-family apartment building had an elevator.

Technology was now feeding upon itself and the structure of life style and the configuration of the cities responded accordingly. The automobile industry combined with the radio communications industry gave birth to a new industry, "advertising". This new industry now set the goals and objectives for all of America! Styles for clothing, food, soap, speech, furniture, housing, appliances, recreation, entertainment, music and every other aspect of culture now became standardized by the new industry. The new medium for this new industry was the radio, newspaper and a new technique called the movies. The silent movies had been entertaining Americans since 1914, but by 1927 the "talking" picture became the main entertainment medium in the U.S., although the radio gained more and more popularity almost daily. By 1930 the U.S. population had reached 122.7 million and one of every five Americans owned an automobile.

With few exceptions it was necessary to live in the "city" to reap all the benefits of these new technological marvels. Only in the city were all the resources available to produce the benefits. The farm did not have the electric power or the transportation systems needed to support the new technologies. Although new technologies of mechanization had increased agricultural production to feed the urban centers, little of the affluence resulting from the industrialization of the urban centers returned to the farm as a reward for this increased contribution of food and fiber. Life on the farm remained hard and forlorn, although far fewer people were needed to produce the food and fiber needed by industry in the cities. The surplus farm populations combined with the demands for labor in the urban centers resulted in massive migrations to the cities. Even though the urban centered industries quickly absorbed the labor supplied by this rural migration, the technical and social fabric of the cities was ill prepared to accept such rapid increases in population. America's traditions of unlimited water supplies, endless forest and rich farmlands obscured any question that these resources might be limited or over taxed by such tremendous increases in population densities. Residential requirements for reasonable density of dwellings, adequate ventilation, fire protection, windows, heating and plumbing did not exist as a practical matter. Most of the Railroad Apartments of New York City in the 1920s had no windows and plumbing was in most cases a single toilet at the end of the hall serving four or five apartments. One interesting omission for all of the row housing built near the automotive plants in Detroit was the absence of any space for the parking of an automobile except in the alley at the rear of the lot or at the curb on the street in front of the house.

Building Codes such as they were, barely touched on these important items and offered little guidance for the design or construction of residential, commercial or industrial buildings. Zoning was also poor to completely lacking and in many central cities skyscrapers began to appear in great profusion set next to each other so close that sunlight was completely cut off and light and fresh air moved between the buildings with difficulty. Massive industrial plants were built with no consideration for adequate fire exits, ventilation, lighting or their impact on the surrounding environment with their noise and smoke and fly ash from the foundries and power plants which burnt high sulfur soft coal.

Industrial waste along with sanitary waste was discharged directly into the storm sewer systems which discharged into the rivers and lakes. Treatment, if any was only a token. America's rivers, lakes and tidal basins became open sewers.

In many towns and cities the industrial plants became the focal points of development for the urban centers. The residential, commercial and institutional (schools, hospitals, etc.) developments oriented themselves around these economic centers of employment and each big city became a conglomeration of these autonomous community centers with a central "city" where the main financial, legal offices, hotels, city officials and large merchants were housed in high rise buildings. The network was tied together with buses or a rail transportation system providing electric street cars for local transportation between neighborhoods and across town; and steam powered trains carrying freight from factory to factory with passengers from the central city to the country or other towns and cities. Most families did not have an automobile before 1930 and by this time the use of horses for transportation had become impractical in the congested cities. Most people walked to work or took a bus or street car, walked to the corner grocery store, the department store, school, the theatre, the doctor, the dentist, etc. The bus or street car was used for that special trip "downtown". School buses were for handicapped children only. Although there were few, if any, personal horse drawn carriages, commercial deliveries were still made with horse drawn wagons throughout the towns and cities. Home deliveries of ice and milk along with trash collections were still being made by horse drawn wagons up to 1941!

In less than a single lifetime after the Civil War, America had moved from a rural based culture to an urban based culture. There was no organized plan for development. Even though substantial portions of the population still lived on the farm, by 1930 it was the urban centers who established the life style and cultural base (standards) for America. It was the collapse of the stock market in October of 1929 and the great depression of 1932 that brought urban development to a painful standstill. Construction of high rise office buildings were stopped overnight with exposed structural steel frames standing naked in mid air. Residential subdivisions completely developed with their streets, sidewalks, sewers and water systems were abandoned with two or three unfinished houses standing as ghostly monuments to a paralyzed economy. The unemployment rate was 25% of the work force. The financial collapse of the economy was exacerbated by the great dust bowls in the midwest that wiped out whatever real economic base (topsoil) that remained for these farms. The population was devastated, the economy was stagnant and the cities were deteriorating.

The federal government stepped into the economic maelstrom with measures and programs that changed the course of urban development for years to come. Beginning with sweeping changes in the nations banking system intended to rescue the bankrupt economy, public works projects were started on a massive scale to put vast numbers of unemployed men back to work. Although these programs were started on very short notice because of the emergency, the administrative structures and concepts of the programs, e.g. construction of streets, new sewers, schools, etc., set the direction for urban and industrial development for the next fifty years. One of the most important of these measures was the establishment of the Rural Electrification Administration whose goal was to electrify the farms of America. Within twenty five years which included the W.W. II years of 1941-45, any amount of electric power became available practically anywhere in the United States. This development more than any other started the dispersion and fragmentation of America's urban centers. During this same period steam powered belt driven machinery was being replaced by electrical motors, bus duct and electrical unit substations. As the electric power lines stretched all over rural America, the telephone followed close behind so that as the farms became electrified, telecommunications now linked rural America with every urban center in the country and for that matter the world.

The depression notwithstanding, technology continued to grow and expand throughout the depression years of the thirties. Aircraft had now developed beyond military and county fair exhibitions to regular scheduled transportation services. Refrigerators began to replace ice boxes and a new industry was born with the packaging and distribution of frozen food. Every home in America now had a radio and talking movies had become part of the American culture.

Chemistry was introduced to the farm with fertilizers and pesticides changing agriculture with quantum increases in production. Television invented in the late twenties was struggling to enter the market place. The automobile encouraged by the tremendous improvements in the street and highway systems increased its production each year accompanied by corresponding improvements in the petroleum industry. The petroleum industry began to make serious inroads into the home heating industry and the coal bin began to disappear from the American basement. The natural gas industry began to see where they could expand into the suburbs from the urban centers and pipelines began to reach out from the gas and oil fields of Texas and Oklahoma toward the markets of the East and the Midwest.

One of the most significant technological advancements at this time was the introduction of building air conditioning as a major industry. The concept of cooling the air for comfort had been around for some time. This had been accomplished by the railroads by moving volumes of air over packs of ice then to the sealed cars for the comfort of the passengers. Although this primitive technique could reduce the temperature, it could do little or nothing to reduce the humidity of the air and was not very efficient. When Willis Carrier invented the air conditioner in 1911 which utilized the expansion of compressed gasses and the evaporate condenser to discharge unwanted heat, there was no limit to the possibilities of use for this invention. In 1925 the first theatres were air conditioned in New York City and in 1937 the Packard Motor Car Company introduced the first air conditioned automobile. These were just the starter projects for this industry. Within a few years air conditioning would change the entire economic, political and social fabric of the United States. It is difficult to think of what part of life this technological achievement would not affect; especially in the southern and southwestern part of the U.S.

The depression prevailed in spite of these rapid advancements in technology and the emergency measures by the government. Economic relief came only when the clouds of war once again gathered in Europe. In 1939 America became the arsenal of democracy when Adolph Hitler invaded Poland and started W.W. II. This mobilization restored full employment and boosted production to unheard of heights. The depression was finally over. When the

Japanese attacked Pearl Harbor in 1941 America was completely engaged in the war until the defeat of the Axis Powers in 1945. The onset of World War II with its death and destruction of millions of people not only changed the course of all human events, but altered the course of urban development dramatically. Technology had received an enormous impetus from the war. Electronics, chemistry, metallurgy, engineering, rockets and of course the new science, nuclear physics, entered the scene of American industry and commerce and expanded to an unprecedented degree. Of equal importance, existing technology made quantum leaps with new machine tools, manufacturing equipment and new materials. With the advent of printed circuits and the micro chip production not only increased, but became more efficient!

The cities however were sadly neglected by these advancements. Indeed, their problems were only exacerbated by the increased pressure that the production of war materials had put on the services and infrastructure of the cities. Maintenance and repairs suffered sometimes to the point of total breakdowns since only war production facilities received top priority for service, repair and replacement. Housing was one of the most severely impacted with densities increasing as much as six hundred percent over normal allowances. Under such circumstances plumbing would break down on a regular basis and domestic kitchens could not keep up with serving meals 24 hours a day to accommodate the three shifts at all of the defense plants. Some of the boarding houses operated like the boarding houses of the gold rush days in Alaska and California. It was at this time that women entered the work force in massive numbers to replace the 11 million men who had been drafted into the armed forces. Massive demographic shifts also took place in the U.S. to make up the needed labor pools for the wartime industries. California which had been known for its big trees, oranges and movies, now became one of the prime production centers for the aircraft industry and Rosie the Riveter became an American legend since she had the perfect touch placing rivets in aluminum air frames.

In 1934 the U.S. Department of Agriculture in its effort to "save the farms", had subsidized the cotton industry by paying the farmers, ranchers and plantation owners not to raise cotton. While this was very profitable for the investors of the cotton industry, it created one of the greatest unemployment surges in the history of the country. With no cotton to pick, tens of thousands of men and women were out of work and on welfare. With the advent of the war they moved North to the great urban centers of St. Louis, Chicago, Detroit, Cleveland, Pittsburgh, New York and Washington, D.C. None of these large cities were ready to cope with such massive migrations in such a short period of time. Schools, hospitals, transportation facilities, police and fire departments had to make rapid adjustments to accommodate the influx of the new migrants. Notwithstanding such changes the world was astounded at the what the U.S. was able to produce during the war years. Even the experts had not expected such enormous amounts of production. Food, airplanes, munitions, guns, clothing, ships, tanks, trucks and fuel were produced in such quantities that even the enemy refused to believe their own intelligence communications about the amounts of war materials crossing the Atlantic and Pacific. Even though much of the German war equipment was superior to the American, e.g. the Tiger tank and the 88 mm cannon, the vast numbers of tanks and bombers from the American arsenal eventually overwhelmed the German armies. This great superiority of resources and the introduction of a new age for mankind with the dropping of the atomic bomb ended the war. Neither the cities or the people would ever be the same again.

The legacy of W.W. II was profound. American capacity for production was at its height and quickly converted from war materials to consumer goods. Automobiles, refrigerators, appliances and many other hard goods had not been manufactured for four years. Other domestic needs had not been met and the pent up demand for clothing, shoes, furniture and many other goods kept the factories humming. Many of the women who had entered the work force during the war did not return to the home and kitchen when the war was over. They had become a permanent part of the work force. This not only altered family life styles, but it substantially changed consumer economics. The conclusion of the war introduced another military concept that impacted the economy and the culture for years to come. This was the Cold War which started with the Soviet Union within months after the war was over. Most importantly for the cities, none of the war mobilization plants were closed or decommissioned. In fact, new industries were started with the introduction of the inter continental missile systems and the nuclear powered submarines. Each Trident submarine with its arsenal of nuclear Polaris missiles carries more explosive power than all of the explosive power that was detonated in W.W. II. As far as the towns and cities were concerned the cost of maintaining such an expensive military posture drained enormous amounts of tax dollars from the needed maintenance and replacements of the nation's infrastructure.

The treaties of unconditional surrender which ended W.W. II also planted the seeds of the multi-national corporation in America. With the English, French, Russian, Polish, Dutch, Belgium as well as the German, Italian and Japanese economies devastated by the war, it was the American resources, money and manpower that filled the breech to resurrect the economies of the free world and its former enemies. Along with the new markets opened up for American industry, especially automobiles, American markets now opened up for European and Japanese industries. In fact, to compensate for the treaty prohibition of standing armies and navies for the German and Japanese powers, the Americans provided for their "defense" and guaranteed to absorb any of their surplus production to support their economies! It was unthinkable to imagine German or Japanese armies with atomic weapons. This combined with great improvements in the transportation industry, the very low wage rates of foreign manufacturers and the constant increases in American wage rates soon shifted the sourcing of manufactured goods from America to Europe and the Orient. Bicycles and sewing machines from Japan, typewriters from Italy, steel from Germany, cameras, television and radios from Japan soon took over the market in part or in total throughout America. The economic impact on America was not readily apparent. Industries still flourished and prospered although the frequencies of government bail-outs increased. Some automobile companies were allowed to go down the tubes, namely Packard and Studebaker, but the slack was picked up by the other car builders. Others however, were not so ignored because of their "requirements for defense". Lockheed and Boeing aircraft manufacturers were repeatedly "assisted" with their cost overruns and the subsidy of the nations railroads on an annual basis was so old hat that it was rarely mentioned in the press.

Even with this substantial shift in sourcing, technology old and new, was advancing at an accelerating pace. With electricity now available at every point on the map in the U.S., the telephone was now commonplace in just about every home and place of business in the country. By the 1950s the "iceman" had become an anachronism and practically every home in America had a refrigerator with its companion freezer. The frozen food industry expanded to meet this opportunity. By 1960 the air conditioning industry had made significant inroads into the automobile and residential markets. In most parts of the U.S. new homes without air conditioning were difficult to sell. In the South air conditioning was mandatory for all of the transferees relocated from the North. The first computers using high heat producing vacuum tubes and large amounts of office space demanded air conditioning so that their tapes and copious amounts of paper would not bind up the machines. Soon new office building designs with non operating windows made air conditioning mandatory. By 1965 it was difficult to sell a car without air conditioning. It is no coincidence that the cities of Houston, Dallas, Atlanta and Los Angeles began rapid expansion when air conditioning was included for any planning and/or building for the South. The South was truly rising again with this air conditioned vitality. And why not? Once the problem of oppressively high temperatures was economically resolved, it was found that the South had everything to offer modern industry and modern living. This was especially true for the absence of traditional northern winter conditions of freezing temperatures and copious amounts of snow. Added to this was the extended growing season for flowers and green grass and in particular the long golf season which lasted from March through November and even sometimes December. Not only the South but even arid deserts of the Southwest reaped this magnificent benefit. The former deserts of southern California, Nevada and Arizona were transformed into year around gardens for working, living and industrial development.

The completion of the Interstate Freeway system in 1972 along with the use of the jet engine for airline travel reduced travel and transportation between cities to a matter of hours compared to the days and weeks before W.W. II. Soon television invaded practically every household in the country and what was portrayed on the TV was soon setting the standard for everything from clothing, food, restaurants, housing, recreation and entertainment. One important TV feature was that whereas the movies of the 30s, 40s and 50s tended to show the city as the center of culture and the good life, the TV tended to show the countryside as the good life and the city as the poor side of the culture with its crowded conditions, violent crime rates, and proliferation of slums.

One of the most significant technological advancements of the post war years in the U.S. was the National System of Interstate Highways. Authorized by the Congress in 1944, recognizing the military value of highways, over 41,000 miles of interstate freeways were constructed in place by 1972. In addition to the vast improvement in automobile and truck transportation between the states, the ease and convenience of mobility between urban centers and the rural countryside between cities, was unprecedented. One could drive from the city of Detroit to Flint, Michigan faster and safer in 1972 than it would have taken to drive across the city of Detroit in 1952. Not only could one completely traverse the urban centers via the freeways, but practically all of rural America was now within convenient commuting distance of the cities.

In the same period commercial aviation logged more passenger miles traveled than ever before. Passenger air terminals now exceeded in size and convenience any railroad terminal ever built. By 1970 any point in the U.S. could be reached by air within a matter of hours. Trans Atlantic flights no longer provided "sleeping" accommodations as they did in the 1950s. Of course the jet engine was the mainspring of this dramatic improvement in air transportation. It is also noteworthy that today, 1996, along with the millions of miles of commercial aviation traveled each year, private airplane travel now exceeds the number of miles traveled by scheduled airlines. It is not even uncommon today for some people to commute every day from their homes to their jobs by private airplane.

In the period from 1945 to 1975 underground America was changed because of the technological improvements in construction machinery and equipment. One of the least known, but of utmost importance, was the construction of thousands of miles of pipelines which now move hundreds of millions of cubic feet of natural gas and petroleum products daily from their point of origin to homes and factories almost everywhere in America. Fuel, a most basic necessity for any industrialized economy is now available at practically any point in the United States. Along with this network of underground piping, water and sewer lines also extend for hundreds of miles beyond the confines of the old urban centers. The city of Detroit Water and Sewer system along with the Consumers Power Gas Co. now serves not only Detroit with its population of 1 million, but the entire southeast Michigan region of 5 million people.

In the post war years the U.S. enjoyed a relatively stable economy and the acquisitiveness of the American consumer was intense to say the least. What had before been classified as luxuries soon became essential to the life style of practically every American. By 1950 it was an anomaly to find in all but the most remote locations, a house without a telephone, radio, refrigerator, indoor plumbing and cooking range with oven. In 1995 most homes have at least two or more telephones, central heating and air conditioning, two or more television sets, VCRs, two to five radios, freezers, dishwashers, garbage disposers, microwaves, washing machines and dryers and in many homes, the Personal Computer. It is said that today, 1997, there are more computers in the country than there are television sets! Of course this would include all of the computers in the work place as well as the home. Other items that are not uncommon in todays home are the Xerox copy machine, the FAX machine, the portable phone and an automobile telephone.

When the Rural Electrification Administration began to electrify the farms of America in 1934, the intent was to bring the electric light and the radio to the farm. No one dreamed of mechanizing the farm or providing electric power for industry. This program was so successful that today, 1997, except for the most remote areas of the desert or the mountains, electric power is available in unlimited quantities. Agriculture, the dominant industry in rural America is now completely electrified and any industry that wishes to locate a new facility in the rural part of the country can ask to day not if, but when their power demands will be met at their new location. Contrasted with the limited availability of electric power in rural areas in the 1920s and the 1930s, the ability of industry to locate where their cost are low and their markets are conveniently and profitably located nearby, is unlimited today.

Although there was a radio in practically every home in 1935, the impact on American lifestyle was small compared to the influence of television on today's culture. Not only are news and historic events instantly portrayed in the living room, but it is difficult to find a single industry that has not changed or at least been dramatically influenced by television. Politics and even international affairs are now "television" directed according to many analyst and it remains to be seen if the benefits of this outstanding technological accomplishment will outweigh some of the disadvantages. What is conspicuously evident is the continuous graphic portrayal of lifestyle for good or ill in the cities, the country and in different regions of the country. Newscast are televised all over the nation on the hour and the half hour for twenty four hours a day. Soap operas, entertainment shows and movies provide a non stop illustration of the type of house to live in, the food to eat, the clothes to wear and even the proper language to speak. the desire for change and "rising expectations" is universal and constantly fueled by television and it all takes place in the home.

By the 1980s air-conditioning had completely changed the composition of American cultural development. The most obvious change has been demographical. With the introduction of air-conditioning to the automobile, the home, school, offices, retail stores and now even in manufacturing plants, life in the sun-belt in the summertime is today a comfortable and even a pleasant experience. This attractive addition to the way we work and live is readily available anywhere electric power is available and as a practical matter, this is anywhere in the United States. No longer do people eschew a trip South during the summer. Even the tourist traffic for fun and recreation is increasing every year throughout the southern part of the country. No longer treated as the luxury it once was in the immediate post war years, air-conditioning is now viewed as essential to building construction in the South as heating and ventilation is essential to buildings in the North.

Not since the Civil War has the South and the southwest witnessed such increases in population and for the first time the development of major commercial and manufacturing industries have expanded in the sun-belt to replace cotton fields and sagebrush. While northern states have been losing population in the 1970s, 1980s and 1990s, the southern states have been making substantial gains. Air conditioning has reached deep into the fabric of American industry. Many jobs which heretofore were burdened with intolerable conditions of heat and humidity during the summer months, are now reasonable and of course much more efficient with the addition of cool and tempered air. From the truck driver, machine operator and farm tractor to the executive office, working conditions are not only more pleasant in the summertime, but in most cases even more efficient than in the winter time! Since Willis Carrier gave us air conditioning in 1911, it took over forty years of development of the main product line and the market itself; but today air-conditioning is an essential part of American life. It may not be too far fetched to say that air-conditioning will have a greater impact on the South than the cotton gin! It is also very significant that the impact of this machine is just now being felt throughout the world, especially in the tropical areas of the new world, Africa and Asia.

In these years after W.W. II it sometimes seems that new technology is moving on the world like a tidal wave. Everything from the "invention" of sliced bread by Wonder bakeries which made the automatic toaster a fixture in the kitchen, to the invention of the instant copy machine for the office and library in the 1960s added increasing momentum to the change of American business practices and our life style in the home. The new age for the end of the 20th century is being called the "Information Age". The computer industry working with the micro chip and the continuing development of solid state physics had set off an information explosion the like of which has not been seen since the invention of the printing press. Coupled with the telephone, FAX machine, Xerox machine, space communication satellites and television, we now have a proliferation of knowledge and instant replays of any event at any time all over the world and even in space. The first landing on the moon was witnessed live by the entire world! From the confines of our homes and automobiles we can now monitor every event almost as soon as it happens. This includes everything from traffic conditions, school board decisions, federal, state and municipal government actions, to weather forecast and international crises. Since good news is rarely broadcast, all the bad news about the urban centers is televised for 24 hours a day.

Just as we experienced the agricultural revolution which was followed by the industrial revolution we are now told that we are experiencing the third wave or the revolution created by the "information age". Cities as well as all other aspects of life were influenced and changed by the first two revolutions, but the jury is still out for us to know to what extent the information age will affect our lives and the future of our cities. Technology was the engine that drove the agricultural and the industrial revolutions and it is again technology that is driving the "information age", but it remains to be seen if the cornucopia that was produced by agriculture and industry can be continued and expanded by the computers and data processors of the new age of information.

Productivity, is that ubiquitous measurement of the amount, valued in dollars, that a worker produces in a given hour, using computers, complex machinery, telecommunication equipment, or a hammer, wrench, or one's head and hands, working alone or with a team at home, in a store, office or factory. This measurement along with other economic indicators, e.g. number of housing starts, number of unemployed and number of employed, number of automobiles, refrigerators, TVs, etc. is some indication of the standard of living we are enjoying and how much the country is growing. Productivity is a direct product of technology combined with man's ingenuity. With no productivity, or with very poor productivity, our standard of living not only does not improve, it may well evaporate.

From 1870 to 1940 productivity in the U.S. did not improve much notwithstanding all of the inventions and discoveries that took place in that time. Although technology had delivered to us many improvements that heretofore had not even been dreamed of, the new techniques and machines were not readily incorporated into the mainstream of commerce and industry. Correspondingly, the bulk of the population did not reap the benefits of these new ideas and conveniences. This seventy year hiatus was also burdened with one of the worst depressions in history. As noted before many changes took place with the urban scene, but little was done to improve the standards for the vast bulk of the population for the simple reason that it took too much investment in time, labor and money to produce more goods for more people. Thousands of new towns were created and then abandoned in this period and the large urban centers reached population densities in excess of all reasonable limits.

Productivity changed dramatically in 1940. As the U.S. mobilized for the war in Europe every bit of technology that was available was put to the task of increasing production. With this mobilization machines and men were combined in the most efficient production machines ever created. After a slight dip in 1945 at the end of the war, productivity again increased with major increases in the Gross National product. All of this meant more jobs and a higher standard of living for most everyone. With these increased standards mobility increased much to the detriment of the major urban centers. When the war ended in 1945 there was a tremendous demand for goods and services to make up for the depression years and the war years. With this vast increase in the mobility of the work force and the customers, almost all new manufacturing factories and process plants with their offices were built in rural America!

CHAPTER 7

THE AUTOMOBILE & THE FRAGMENTATION OF CITIES

A lthough many events and technological changes have influenced and changed the urban centers, none has been more conspicuous or more profound than the automobile. Not only has the use of the automobile, truck and farm tractor changed our pattern of living to the point of no return, but the industry of producing, selling and operating the car has become a critical part of the economy. Some 15 million Americans have jobs (1985) directly related to the automobile industry. The desire and need for some form of transportation (other than walking) goes back to ancient times. For thousands of years the only form of transportation was by foot. The fastest speed about ten miles an hour. With the domestication of the horse about seven thousand years ago, this speed was increased to about thirty five miles an hour. By the beginning of the 20th century the speed of the horse had been surpassed by the railway locomotive which could travel up to 120 miles per hour and by the middle of the century even this has been surpassed by the automobile. Of course we must also note that air travel and space travel exceed speeds of hundreds and even thousands of miles per hour. Yet, except for the horse, the ox cart and the ocean going ship, practically nothing was achieved until the 19th century with the advent of the steam engine and finally the automobile with the internal combustion engine.

The automobile got started in Europe. A French physicist, Sadi Carnot (1796-1832) described an ideal engine that could transform heat into work. The reciprocating steam engine, developed by the Scottish engineer James Watt (1736-1819), utilized the expansion of steam for the production of mechanical work. Steam powered cars were not uncommon in England as early as 1830, but eventually these were defeated by the combined interest of the harness makers and the stage coaches who got legislation passed that made it impossible for the steam cars to operate. Although steam cars could operate fairly well, they had another problem that they were burdened with; they occasionally blew up. In the 1860s a French engineer, Jean J. Lenoir (1822-1900), built the first practical gas engine. Lenoir produced small quiet gas engines and the internal-combustion engine became a commercial success. Many of Lenoir's engines were installed in factories. This was soon followed by a German, Nicolaus Otto, who invented the basic four-cycle internal combustion engine in 1876. Another German, Karl Friedreich Benz (1844-1929), built the first reliable internal-combustion engine automobile in 1885. It was a motorized tricycle. The car was equipped with a single cylinder four stroke engine. It had electric instead of flame ignition and there was a differential gear. In addition, the engine was water cooled. Benz even had a rudimentary radiator to cool the water for reuse. All of these three ideas were original with Benz and are on practically all of the 100 million cars and trucks in the U.S. today! Benz was convinced that the internal-combustion engine would replace the horse and revolutionize the world's transportation system. He worked on his vehicle in the face of many obstacles including the lack of money and the fact that many of his friends thought he was a little unbalanced. After many trials he sold his first car to a Parisian named Rogers in 1887. By 1888 he employed 50 workmen to build his tricycle car and in 1890 started to build a four wheeler. Gottlieb Daimler developed a superior single cylinder engine that he fitted to a bicycle producing the first motorcycle. Daimler built his first car in 1886 with four wheels. Daimler and Benz eventually merged in 1926 under the name of Mercedes-Benz. Very soon the French were designing, building and selling cars in small numbers, mostly to rich people. They built luxurious, but fairly reliable vehicles well adapted to the ancient hard surfaced roads that connected their cities. Many of these were exported to America. Early on America's "horseless carriage" became known by the French word, "automobile".

Thoughts of mechanical propulsion occurred early in the U.S.. A patent issued by George Washington in April 25, 1794 to John Staples of New York covers "the construction of carriage to be propelled by mechanical powers." It was never built, but this was a beginning in America. In 1787 Oliver Evans built a steam powered vehicle called the "Oruktor Amphibilow", it worked, as an automobile and as a paddle wheel boat! However, it was in 1893 that Charles E. and Frank Duryea offered a four wheeled motor wagon to the public in Springfield, Massachusetts. The flimsy car with its one-cylinder engine gave a poor showing on its first ride, but in 1896 the Duryea Motor Wagon Company produced its third car and from these plans 13 more cars were built. But it was Ransom E. Olds, truly the first automobile manufacturer in the modern sense of the word, who put up a plant in Lansing, Michigan in 1899. The plant was dedicated to manufacturing "Merry Oldsmobiles." In 1900 Olds shipped 1400 Merry Oldsmobiles and by 1904 he had shipped another 10,000. By 1908 there were 485 different companies producing horseless carriages in the U.S. In 1910 along with Halley's Comet streaking across the sky, the automobile industry climbed to $230 million. By 1915 the industry more than doubled compared to 1910 accounting for 35% of consumer durable output. By 1920 this figure was 40%. By 1930 of the 42 million U.S. work force, 12 million owed their jobs directly and indirectly to the automobile. Today, 1995, their are over 100 million cars and trucks on 13 million miles of American streets and highways.

Fathered by the automobile industry, the trucking industry soon became a tour' de force in the transportation of goods and services to rural as well as urban America. The value of the truck first became apparent in W.W. I and its usefulness and efficiency in replacing the horse soon after. Today, trucking not only has replaced the horse, but it has also replaced all but the heaviest loads carried by the railroad. With some 24 million trucks in use today, the distribution network for goods and services in the U.S. is the envy of the world.

The interchangeability of parts, the keystone to mass production, originated with Eli Whitney's manufacturing of muskets for the U.S. Army in 1800. The combination of Whitney's technique with the idea put forth by Henry Ford that the automobile was a "necessity" not a luxury is what created the revolution for the automobile industry. This, not mass production, was Ford's unique contribution. Mass production was an old idea in Ford's time. In 1776 Jeremiah Wilkinson had invented the jig, a fixture providing the means of making identical parts in series, over and over again. Whitney perfected this technique by adding the concept of tolerances to the interchangeability of parts for his production of muskets. Soon automobiles and trucks were being produced in quantities never even dreamed of at the turn of the century. In 1915 Ford produced its 1 millionth automobile in Highland Park, Michigan.

The rapid growth of this industry occurred almost exclusively in the urban centers of the country in the 1920s and the 1930s. Most of these manufacturing plants were multi-story built with reinforced concrete. Because of the heavy floor loads and the vertical feed of the conveyor lines which was the latest wisdom at this time for the assembly of automobiles, the old style timber framed wooden mill buildings could not meet the new manufacturing requirements. These huge monoliths soon became part of the urban landscape and although they were built to last a thousand years, they were obsolete very soon after they were built. Other industries, e.g. steel, rubber, textiles, lumber, all required to support the car builders, also located as close to auto plants as possible. They all had the same needs, electric power, clean water supplies, sewers, rail transportation, labor etc., as the assembly plants. In the early part of the 20th century the big city was the only place where these resources were available. Most importantly the product line itself, the automobile, now provided the means for people (the labor supply) to get to work without depending on public transportation! People could now live many miles away from their jobs. The labor force was now "mobile" **and could live anywhere they chose as long as they could afford the gas to get them to work. This was the real birth of the suburb.**

Along with the growth of the automobile industry in the 1920s, 1930s and even the 1940s, the automobile itself was the primary means of transferring the rural population of America to the urban centers of the nation. Ironically, the automobile in the 1960s, 1970s, 1980s and the 1990s has become the primary means by which Americans are moving back from the urban centers to the rural parts of the country. To a great extent, the work that people do, processing information, has moved with them to their homes or to the small "Office Park". Notwithstanding the popular hyperbole of the 70s, 80s and the 90s, from those who lament the abandonment of the urban centers by major industries, the heavily subsidized mass transit systems, e.g. subways, buses, monorails, etc. could not reverse the exodus from the cities since none of these government systems can match the cost, comfort or efficiency of the automobile. The automobile is by far the most efficient mass transit system ever devised. Even the argument that the streets and freeways are subsidized is not valid since all of the construction and maintenance of these systems are financed by weight and fuel taxes. The so called fuel crises of 1973 may yet prove to be a blessing in disguise since the automobiles of today are three to five times more efficient than they were in 1973. This industry with its first cousins the truck and farm tractor has done more to lift the yoke of toil from mankind than any other.

Almost anywhere we look today we see the impact and the influence of the automobile. It has completely altered our food supply, our housing, our politics, our military defense, our recreation, our economics and most significantly, our cities. In other words our entire culture. Conspicuous by its almost total absence is the horse. Our entire life revolved around the horse at the turn of the century just as it had for the previous 2,000 years. This included of course not only the barns to shelter the animals, the carriages and farm equipment and their feed and fodder, but also the very substantial amount of land dedicated to pasture and raising hay for feed. All of these facilities and especially the land now became available for other crops when the tractors, trucks and cars replaced the horse. The American farm now became much more productive and incidentally, more land was now available for urban expansion!

As the farms became more efficient and the automobile industry needed more labor, surplus manpower left the farm and moved to the urban centers for work. These were major demographic shifts from the farms to the cities. The automobile and of course the road system that had to accompany it also brought more reliable transportation to labor, industry and the consumer. The weather no longer restricted travel the way it did with the horses. It wasn't perfect, but automobile heaters and paved roads were a tremendous improvement over the mud tracks and open air wagons and carriages. Such major changes also brought new economics to America. As the horse trader, feed store, buggy whip manufacturers and the blacksmith faded into obscurity, the car dealership, used car lot, gas station, bump shop and bridge and highway departments emerged. Automobiles traveled very poorly over the dirt roads of rural America and few if any of the old bridges could carry the new truck loadings. All told this new economy amounted to no less than 10% and sometimes as much as 25% of the gross national product.

As the entire transportation system became more efficient, the American landscape changed. New paved roads, streets, and bridges replaced the old dirt and gravel roads along the section lines of rural and urban America. These were accompanied by something else that was new, traffic control signs and signals. With these also came the traffic policeman and the new rules of the road which included speed limits, weight taxes, and driver's licenses. As more and more people felt the freedom of the road, safety became a bigger problem and the emergency wards of the hospitals increased their business many times over. This new technology did not come without its problems. Other changes in the landscape included the drive-in theatre, the strip shopping center and the bill-board on the barns, buildings and highways. Recreation now became a major industry with the automobile. Previously recreation had been pretty much con-fined to the church picnics, horse shoe tournaments and Sunday concerts at the town square or the summer resort at the beach that could be reached by the railroad. With the automobile recreation horizons were limited only by the ex-tent of the highway systems. This brought out the motel industry, the fast food restaurants, state park systems, ski resorts and a multiplicity of summer and winter resorts that could not be reached by the rail roads. The political frame-work of the country also changed. The State Highway Department, the County Road Commission and the Municipal Department of Streets and Railways be-came one of the most important parts of the American scene. Snow removal, storm drainage, bridge maintenance and pavement maintenance were essential to the transportation system.

The diet and food habits of America changed with the coming of the truck and automobile. Up to W.W. I fresh fruits and vegetables were pretty much a seasonal or summer delicacy. Some commercial canning and a great deal of home canning with cool storage in the fruit cellar preserved this produce through the winter months. Meat, which on the farm was salted, dried or smoked in the smoke house, was made available at the local butcher shop or not at all for the urban dweller. In the home this food was preserved in the "ice box" until it was consumed. The ice box held 25 to 100 pounds of ice which was replaced every two to four days during the summer. During the winter a window box was often used. Although the first railroad refrigerator cars were built in Detroit in 1866 and by 1875 refrigerator cars were used regularly to ship meat from the Midwest stockyards to the East, it was not until 1937 that the U.S. had 2 million domestic refrigerators, but of equal importance, refrigerator trucks were common place and fresh meat and fish were now being shipped all over the country for 12 months of the year. After W.W. II the ice box had become an antique and the ice man had disappeared completely. In addition, the freezer had become part of the American lexicon and the frozen food industry was now a major part of the market place. Semi tractor trailer rigs now moved frozen meat, fish, vegetables and pre-cooked dinners from the factories to the supermarkets. In addition, refrigerated produce and fruit is moved from Florida, Texas and Arizona to New York and Chicago all year around.

Although it is difficult to say that any one change from the automobile is more important than another, one result seems to stand out more than any of the others. As automobiles became an essential part of our life style instead of a luxury (this is what Henry Ford wanted!), the towns and cities of America were "Too Small" to accommodate them! At first it was thought that the horseless carriage would take up the same space in the barns and carriage houses that had been occupied by the horse and carriage. This was certainly true in the rural parts of the country, but in the urban areas it was a different story. In the first place most of the people in the urban areas did not own a horse, carriage or a carriage house. Only people in the upper income brackets owned such wealth. Most urban dwellers lived in multi-family housing and relied on public transportation to get to their jobs or recreation areas. When any of these people could afford a new (or used) car, they either parked on the street or in many cases moved to the suburbs where there was more space or even a garage to park the car. Owning and keeping a car was just too expensive for the average income family in the American city. In addition, in the large urban centers a car wasn't all that necessary. Public transportation, street cars, subways, buses and even inter-urban, were adequate to move people to their jobs and home again. Since a great deal of the housing, multi-family, row housing, etc., was located close to the factories, mills and foundries, walking was about the most economical transportation and tremendous numbers of people, especially the new immigrants, relied on their feet to control cost. It is noteworthy that an enormous amount of row housing built in the 1920s in Detroit, Cleveland and Chicago had the houses so close together that a car could not fit in a driveway between the houses and multi-family housing had no provisions at all for automobiles. In these cases parking in the street at the curb could no way accommodate a car for every dwelling unit in the apartment building although in some cases garages were available from the alleys in the rear. All of this housing became obsolete when the car became a necessity instead of a luxury as Henry Ford had predicted.

When mass production reduced the price of a new car to 16% of the average annual income (new Ford for $360.00, circa 1926) and a used car for less than $100.00, everything in the urban centers changed. Almost everyone had a car even if they didn't need one. Come hell or high water you had to have a car! As Will Rogers said at the depths of the depression in 1932, with things as bad as they were, we were the only country in the world where everyone would go to the poor house in his own automobile. The cities could just not handle this new invasion of one to two ton behemoths for each family that lived in the city. There just wasn't enough room. Incidentally, if everyone had a horse and wagon at this time, there wouldn't have been enough room either. Superimposed on this basic fact, not enough square feet of space to accommodate a car for everyone, were a host of new problems never before experienced with the horses. Speed limits, the cars were much faster than the horses, traffic controls, automobile accidents , noise and the most obstreperous if not incorrigible problem, parking. The suburbs soon sprouted to absorb the overflow from the major urban centers. Since most of their incorporated land area was dedicated to "new" subdivisions which included plenty of space for automobiles, the major traffic and space requirements did not create the incorrigible problems that had taken over the big cities. The suburbs did well during the post war years after W.W. II while the big urban centers suffered more and more for not recognizing the very demanding requirements of the automobile.

Economist have debated for years the causes for the rise and fall of the major urban centers. Conquest, disease, increases in capital to labor ratios, increases in the size of the labor force and improvements in technology, all have been cited for the variation in the growth or decline of the cities. In these modern times, few if any, have recognized the tremendous impact of technology and in particular, the automobile.

The modern big city is the result of technology's ability to move people. In 19th century London everyone walked to work except the owners who lived over their shops and stores. By the middle of that century people began to acquire wheels. First it was the railroad, then the streetcar, the bicycle, the subway and then the automobile and the electric elevator. It was this ability to move people that made possible the large operations and organizations, businesses, hospitals, universities and government agencies. By 1914 every technical means of moving people to and from an office or a manufacturing center in a large city, had been developed.

As a practical matter the automobile has created a new city to replace the obsolete urban center. These new cities are better known today as Metropolitan Detroit, Metropolitan Chicago, Metropolitan Houston, Metropolitan Atlanta, Metropolitan Los Angeles, etc. No political boundaries have been established for these new cities, since the legislatures and the legal systems have not yet caught up to our new technology. Some metropolitan districts have been established to provide sewer service, public water supplies and even some police services, even these have been severely restricted from operating at their peak potential because of the old political boundaries. Except for the Interstate Freeways, the streets, bridges and roads have fared poorly under this fragmented system. Practically all of today's towns and cities were established in the 18th and 19th century. In other words the political boundaries, the streets and most all of the infrastructure for all of these towns was established in the horse and buggy days and even today have not completely adjusted to the automobile. The bigger the urban center, the more difficult the adjustment. Some of the newer suburban communities, e.g. Troy, Michigan, North of Detroit, have adapted quite well to the automobile. Troy was designed and built out in the last two decades of this century and appears to be moving into the 21st century with a full appreciation of today's technology including the automobile. Rigid requirements for parking are imposed on all new construction, including residential, and all parking at all of the industrial and commercial office buildings and retail stores is free! Most importantly, any town or city that ignores automobile requirements will not prevail for any length of time.

At this time, 1996, the most conspicuous growth of the automobile market in the U.S. is for a 3rd car for every family. Most commonly this third vehicle is a four wheel drive van, pick-up truck, a recreation vehicle or tractor. Although the metropolitan areas have adjusted fairly well to the two car family, the addition of a third vehicle has undoubtedly created some problems for some, but in the rural areas being developed this appears to be the norm.

CHAPTER 8

NUCLEAR POWER AND URBAN DEVELOPMENT

One of the most significant technological advancements in the last 50,000 years was the discovery and use of nuclear power. On July 16, 1945 the first atomic bomb was exploded over the desert in New Mexico, heralding the beginning of the Atomic Age. This is the first discovery of a new source of energy since the invention of the water wheel or for that matter since the discovery of fire itself. When the first nuclear powered submarine made the first trip under the polar ice pack over the North Pole and across the arctic ocean, the importance of this kind of power staggered the imagination. Like fire however, this new blessing is a two edge sword. Used as a weapon it poses the threat of the extinction of mankind on earth. Used properly it can be mankind's salvation with increased food production, elimination of air and water pollution, new medical services and most importantly, new cities and towns. The military use of this energy now dominates national and international peacetime development, but research for peaceful uses continues at a slow pace. Whether for war or for peace, the impact of nuclear energy on urban development will be profound. Some cities will fade away and some new towns will be created.

The double edged sword of nuclear power will shape the future of urban development for years to come. Not only in the United States, but all over the world and for that matter on the moon and other planets. On the one hand the military use of this new form of energy as a weapon will dictate the shape, cost and most importantly, the location of our future towns and cities. On the other hand this new form of energy and power will enable our towns and cities to be located almost anywhere we chose. No longer is urban development restricted to those parts of the country where natural water supplies and urban services are conveniently located. Electrical energy up to this time has been pretty much restricted to 250 or even 300 miles from power generation plants, will now be available anywhere with the proper installation of an atomic power plant. Not-withstanding this advantage, no power plant of any kind should be located with-in one hundred miles of an urban center.

The new weapons of war including nuclear war heads and their missile delivery systems must first be understood to appreciate why new urban develop-ments should not be located at or near our major urban centers. For the last fifty years during the cold war the threat of nuclear attack was focused on the U.S. and the Soviet Union. Since the collapse of the Soviet Union the pressure on the U.S. was relieved for a while only to be rekindled again with the recent sabre rattling of China. China, the largest nation on earth along with India, are also a nuclear powers. As we know from the history of weapons development, any weapon system all too soon becomes commonplace with all of the nations and all of the armies of the world. In 1950 only the U.S. and the Soviets had nuclear weapons. Today, fifty years later, nuclear weapons and their delivery systems are part of the regular military arsenal of Great Britain, France, China, India and probably Pakistan. Other countries which probably have these weapons because they are so easy to build, are Israel, Argentina, and Iran. As a practical matter almost anyone can build a nuclear device, but substantial resources are needed to build the delivery systems.

A common trend in the history of weapons has been the development of smaller, more efficient and more economical reproductions of the basic proto-type. Whether we see the English long bow developed from the original com-pound bows of the Levant, or the sophisticated M-16 rifle whose origins go back to the massive artillery piece fielded by the Turks in the 14th century, each generation of development has been to make the piece smaller and more eco-nomical. Nuclear weapons are following the same pattern. Since so many coun-tries in the world now have nuclear weapons along with nuclear power, it is safe to assume that design and development are moving at as rapid a pace as ever. The only reason the weapons have not so far been used it would appear is the threat of mutual assured destruction (MAD) and the expense of building and maintaining the delivery systems. This rationale is valid with organized govern-ments or resistance movements. The irrational terrorist is another matter and no doubt is of grave concern for all reasonable nations.

As we have seen, technological advancements in weapons have closely paralleled the over all trends of technological improvements in general. It comes as no surprise that the history of weapons development follows this pattern very closely. Correspondingly, the rate of change and improvements in weapons technology has increased dramatically in recent years. In reviewing this history and in particular the impact of weapons on the evolution of cities, the current state of the art offers some insight into the future evolution and growth of the cities in America. Although the early catapult and the trebuchet had a major impact on the design of the early cities, it was gunpowder and the development of artillery that had the most significant influence on the design and configuration of the city in the middle ages. The most conspicuous change was the elimination of the "city wall" and/or the obsolescence of the feudal castle with its ramparts and drawbridge. Port cities also changed their design to provide shore batteries for defense and protection from the guns of their naval adversaries. Conventional artillery using gunpowder propellants was in one sense merely an extension or improvement over the basic catapult substituting gunpowder for the recoil energy of the flexible timbers used to launch the stones. Note that the "stones" were still in use for the cannon well into the 19th century long after iron balls were introduced along with percussion fuses on explosive shells.

Aviation in W.W. I added the third dimension to modern warfare. This relatively new technology provided a new delivery system for bombs and ballistics missiles to the enemy. The Spanish Civil War and finally W.W. II saw this system brought to a state of near perfection with the delivery of thousands of tons of explosives not only to enemy armies, but also to towns and cities with no distinction between military or civilian targets. London, Berlin, Dresden, Hamburg, Tokyo and of course, Hiroshima and Nagasaki saw massive destruction. This experience more than any other demonstrated very conclusively that there was no distinction between enemy military targets and enemy towns and cities. The German V-2 rocket however, brought artillery and aviation into a single new delivery system that is the most formidable ever devised. The range of the original V-2 (buzz bomb) was only a few hundred miles and its accuracy left much to be desired. Today, the range of these modern missile delivery systems is global and their inertial guidance systems provide accuracy up to a few meters of their global targets from any launch point on the planet. These delivery systems include the nuclear powered submarines which may launch from any point on the high seas. The submarine Trident missile has a range today of 4,600 miles.

The warheads of these missile systems have also reached the zenith of explosive power that can be achieved, namely, nuclear explosive devices with enormous capabilities for destruction. The warhead of a single Cruise missile carries a nuclear device equivalent to 200,000 tons (a ton is 2,000 lbs) of TNT, or about 15 times bigger than the atom bomb dropped on Hiroshima, Japan in 1945. The range of these short range missiles is about 2,000 miles, but they can be launched from any conventional aircraft carrier, submarine, truck or airplane. In addition, the MIRV intercontinental ballistic missile can speed between continents through space in a few minutes. The MIRV carries several nuclear warheads which are independently launched from the main missile to individual targets after the main missile approaches the general target area. Any of these systems have the ability to obliterate any city or urban center on the face of the earth. No longer can the people of the U.S. believe that they will not be affected by a war in the future. Since 1865 the cities of the U.S. have not even thought of such a question because of the protection of the Atlantic and the Pacific oceans.

Today's technology and the experience of W.W. I & II all but eliminates any mythology about the ethics of warfare. The weapons and the delivery systems are such that the general population cannot be excluded as targets. With a war the entire population will by definition be embraced. Defense concepts notwithstanding, the only real defense to the weapons of today is to not be at the same locations as the targets identified by the weapon's systems. By such a definition any major urban center (primary target) is the place to be avoided when the first, second, third, fourth, etc., missile exchange is fired.

The threat of nuclear war may well go down in history as the greatest deterrent to war in history. For most of history warfare occupied an almost minor role in the affairs of men. That is to say other concerns were more important. The fear of natural disasters, sickness and famine were the most important concerns of daily living throughout most of history. Only in recent times has war assumed the important position in men's affairs that influence our lives on a day to day basis. Although there were great trials and tribulations when the Chaldean, Nebuchadnezzar II conquered the Israelites in 587 B.C. and Alexander conquered the known world by 323 B.C. or Genghis Khan threatened Europe with his conquest of Asia, it was modern warfare that spread world wide terror and changed the way men lived for years afterwards. Napoleon is undoubtedly the originator of the organization of massive armies based on the draft with financing from the income tax. According to some authorities he organized the first military strategies for the use of artillery. The American Civil War was probably the first to employ industrialized equipment in warfare with the use of the railroads for rapid troop deployment and the telegraph for communications across the country. In spite of the heavy casualties in this war World War I followed with even more sophisticated armaments and equipment with 15 million people killed. In this war entire towns and villages were wiped off the face of the earth. In the battle of the Somme in 1916 the British suffered 420,000 casualties, the French 200,000 and the Germans about 450,000. The front was 12 miles long. Never was more than eight miles gained. This was followed 21 years later with 51 million people killed in World War II using even more modern armaments and equipment. Throughout these bleak episodes of human history certain characteristics were common to the various parties engaged in the conflicts.

1. The great wars were started from positions of apparent strength.
2. All offensives were generally launched with superiority of manpower and/or firepower.
3. The wars were invariably directed by "old" men in secure positions out of the line of fire.
4. Modern wars have always been financed by the old men in secure positions out of the line of fire.
5. War materials and their profits were always produced by the old men in secure positions.
6. Wars were always fought by young men. Old men have always been too weak and/or sick, too smart and have always had too much to lose to risk fighting.

7. It has always been believed that warfare would produce substantial gains for the winners.
8. As far as is known, warfare has never been started with the intention of committing suicide.
9. Women, with minor exceptions have never been engaged in combat on the front line of fire.

Studies of nuclear war with computerized models renders all of these items moot!

A very substantial effort has been underway in the U.S. for some years now attempting to discourage any preparations for a nuclear war. The most frustrating part of this effort is that to a considerable extent it is misguided and may even be counter productive if it stimulates the wrong reaction from the people and the government. As Salvado de Madariage came to realize in chairing the League of Nations Disarmament Commission: "Nations don't distrust each other because they are armed; they are armed because they distrust each other." Disarmament therefore may be a mirage which can distract people from the more important issue of ameliorating their real differences. Surely the technology is not going to disappear. If anything it is going to increase, become more economical and widely disseminated.

Professor Martin Hellman of Stanford University is a mathematician who has gained a reputation for his expertise in statistics and probability. Hellman has reached the dismal conclusion that nuclear war is inevitable based on a mathematical process called the "two-step Markov principle." The principle can be explained in terms of Russian Roulette. In Russian roulette one takes a revolver with six chambers and loads only one of the chambers. The six chambered cylinder is then given a forceful spin, then without looking the barrel is placed against the person's brain and the trigger is pulled. There is one chance in six of getting killed. If one plays the game twice, the two chances of being shot reinforce each other and the odds are almost one in three of self destruction. After ten trials the odds are 84% that the person is dead; after 20 trials, 97%. If one continues to play the odds become 100% that death will become inevitable, or a probability of one! Hellman believes that we are playing a continuous game of Russian roulette. He further believes that even total disarmament is not the answer. Our knowledge of how to build nuclear weapons makes disarmament relatively useless. In a conventional war, as soon as one side begins to lose, the weapons would be quickly built by the losing side and the nuclear war would immediately be ignited. Hellman believes that the only solution is the elimination of war of any kind as a method of settling disputes. (Nirvana)

Since the times of the first gatherings of human beings into clans, villages and then towns, the military arts and technology have been the dominant force that has shaped the evolution and configuration of the urban center. Not only has the configuration of the cities been shaped by the state of the military arts, but the very "threat" of military conquest has influenced and directed the design, construction, shape and operation of the urban metropolis. Today, 1996, the year of super power summits, star wars, and a great deal more technology than any single person really understands, the threat of total annihilation is just as strong, maybe even stronger, a motivation force as the conquest of Timurlane across the Levant in 1401 or the Libyans against Leptis Magna 2,000 years ago. Although the media does not express such a threat in such blunt terms, the daily recitation of the international news brings home with graphic illustration the threat of attack on the American homestead. These continuous and sometimes not too subtle threats combined with the other problems of urban living make up a genuine tour-de-force propelling the American population move to the rural countryside. But what is the military threat to urban America?

Scientific and military studies are legion over the last thirty five years analyzing the results of a nuclear attack on the United States from the Soviet Union. One of the best analysis has been the study by the "Office of Technology Assessment" undertaken at the request of the U.S. Senate Committee on Foreign Relations to describe the effects of a nuclear war on the civilian populations, economies and societies of the United States and the Soviet Union. Nuclear war is not a comfortable subject. Throughout all of the variations, there is one continuous theme, a nuclear war would be a catastrophe. A military attack with nuclear weapons, even limited, could be expected to kill people and inflict economic damage on a scale unprecedented in the American experience. A large scale nuclear exchange would be a calamity unprecedented in human history. The following Executive Summary is taken directly from the study:

1. The effects of a nuclear war that cannot be calculated are at least as important as those for which the calculations are attempted. Moreover, even these limited calculations are subject to very large uncertainties. Conservative military planners tend to base their calculations on factors that can either (be) controlled or predicted, and to make pessimistic assumptions. For example, planning for strategic nuclear warfare looks at the extent to which civilian targets will be destroyed by blast, and discounts the additional damage which may be caused by fires that the blast could ignite. This is not because fires are unlikely to cause damage, but because the extent of fire damage depends on factors such as weather and details of building construction that make it much more difficult to predict blast damage. While it is proper for a military plan to provide for the destruction of key targets by the surest means even in unfavorable circumstances, the observer should remember that actual damage will be greater than the military calculations. This is particularly true for indirect effects such as deaths resulting from injuries and the unavailability of medical care or for economic damage resulting from disruption and disorganization rather than from direct destruction. For more than a decade (or twenty years) the declared policy of the United States has given prominence to a concept of "assured destruction". The capabilities of U.S. nuclear weapons have been described in terms of the level of damage they surely inflict even in the most unfavorable circumstances. It should be understood that in the event of actual nuclear war, the destruction resulting from an all-out nuclear attack would probably be far greater. In addition to the tens of millions of deaths during the days and weeks after the attack, there would probably be further millions (perhaps tens of millions) of deaths in the ensuing months or years. In addition to the enormous economic destruction caused by the actual nuclear explosions, there would be some years during which the residual economy would decline further, as stocks (of materials) were consumed and machines wore out faster than recovered production could replace them. Nobody knows

how to estimate the likelihood that industrial civilization might collapse in the areas attacked. Additionally the possibility of significant long term ecological damage cannot be excluded.

2. The impact of even a "small" or "limited" nuclear attack would be enormous. Although predictions of the effects of such an attack are subject to the same uncertainties as predictions of the effects of an all-out attack, the possibilities can be bounded (limitless). OTA examined the impact of a small attack on economic targets (an attack on oil refineries limited to 10 missiles), and found that while economic recovery would be possible, the economic damage and social dislocation could be immense. A review of calculations of the effects on civilian populations and economies of major counterforce attacks found that while the consequences might be endurable (since they would be on a scale with wars and epidemics that nations have endured in the past), the number of deaths might be as high as 20 million. Moreover, the uncertainties are such that no government could predict with any confidence what the results of a limited attack or counterattack would be even if there was no further escalation.

3. It is therefore reasonable to suppose that the extreme uncertainties about the effects of a nuclear attack, as well as the certainty that the minimum consequences would be enormous, both play a role in the deterrent effect of nuclear weapons.

4. There are major differences between the United States and the Soviet Union that effect the nature of their vulnerability to nuclear attack, despite the fact that both are large and diversified industrialized countries. Differences between the two countries in terms of population distribution, closeness of population to other targets, vulnerability of agricultural systems, vulnerability of cities to fire, socioeconomic systems, and political systems create significant asymmetries in the potential effects of nuclear attacks. Differences in civil defense preparations and in the structure of the strategic arsenal compound these asymmetries. By and large, the Soviet Union is favored by geography and by a political-economic structure geared to emergencies; The United States is favored by having a bigger and better economy and (perhaps) a "greater capacity for effective decentralization." (emphasis is

mine.) The larger size of Soviet weapons also means that they are likely to kill more people while aiming at something else.

5. Although it is true that effective sheltering and/or evacuation could save lives, it is not clear that a civil defense program based on providing shelters or planning evacuation would necessarily be effective. To save lives it is not only necessary to provide shelters in, or evacuation to, the right places, it is also necessary to provide food, water, medical supplies, sanitation, security against other people, possibly filtered air, etc.. After fallout diminishes, there must be enough supplies and enough organization to keep people alive while production is being restored. The effectiveness of civil defense measures depends, among other things on the events leading up to the attack, the enemy's targeting policy, and shear luck.

6. The situation in which the survivors of a nuclear attack find themselves will be unprecedented. The surviving nation would be far weaker economically, socially and politically, than one would calculate by adding up the surviving economic assets and the numbers and skills of the surviving people. Natural resources would be destroyed; surviving equipment would be designed to use materials and skills that no longer exist; and indeed some regions might be almost uninhabitable. Furthermore, prewar patterns of behavior would surely change, though in unpredictable ways. Finally, the entire society would suffer from the enormous psychological shock of having discovered the extent of its vulnerability.

7. From an economic point of view, and possibly from a political and social viewpoint as well, conditions after an attack would get worse before they started to get better. For a period of time people could live off supplies left over from before the war. But shortages and uncertainties would get worse. The survivors would find themselves in a race to achieve viability , i.e. production at least equaling consumption plus depreciation, before stocks ran out completely. A failure to achieve viability, or even a slow recovery, would result in many deaths and much additional economic, political and social deterioration. The post war damage could be as devastating as the damage from the actual nuclear explosions.

The study continues in depth to examine a full range of possible nuclear attacks, with attacking forces ranging in extent from a single weapon to the bulk of a superpower's arsenal. The report deals explicitly with both Soviet attacks on the United States and U.S. attacks on the Soviet Union. It addresses the multiple effects of nuclear war, indirect as well as direct, long term as well as short term, and social and economic as well as physical. The cities selected for the model are Detroit, Michigan for the United States and Leningrad for the Soviet Union using one nuclear weapon or ten nuclear weapons. The case studies include attacks on oil refineries, limited to 10 missiles, a Counterforce attack including an attack only on ICBM silos as a variant, and attacks on a range of military and economic targets using large fractions of existing arsenals. Today comparisons to the Soviet Union are moot, but the study is still valid when we substitute "any nation" for the U.S.S.R.

What becomes patently clear from this study, as well as many other studies, is that the major urban centers in this country will be primary targets for nuclear missiles in the next major war or even a limited war! All major urban centers in the U.S. now face the same possible fate as London, Berlin, Dresden, Hamburg, Tokyo, Nagasaki and Hiroshima in the last war. Another obstinate reality is the number and destructiveness of existing nuclear weapons. The United States now has about 30,000 warheads. the Russians had about the same number and since the collapse of the Soviet Union they (the Russians) cannot locate them all from their inventory. In addition, a single U.S. Poseidon submarine can fire 160 independently targetable nuclear warheads, each several times more powerful than the Hiroshima bomb at any Soviet city. This one submarine's weapons can kill 30 million people. The arsenals of many other nations are equally grim.

There are three outstanding disadvantages to any of these weapon systems. First, to maintain and launch any of these missiles is extremely expensive. It is analogous to maintaining a knight in the middle ages. Training the knight started when he was twelve years old. The horses had to be especially bred to carry the knight with his heavy armor. The knight with his horse had to be housed and fed daily, month after month and year after year with continuous practice to maintain his readiness for combat. The feudal system which prevailed for centuries was supported and preserved by this very expensive weapons system. It is noteworthy that when the English bowmen developed the "English Long Bow" and engaged the French at the battle of Crecy in 1346 and again at Agincourt in 1415, the French knights were helpless before the English archers who massacred them with their armor piercing arrows. The bow was one of the most economical weapons ever produced. It cost an English peasant about two months wages. Of course the peasant had to maintain his skill with constant practice. Most importantly, these two battles marked the end of the Feudal system in Europe. An inter-continental ballistic missile (ICBM) system like the knight is also very expensive. It is made up of very expensive hardware(warheads and delivery systems), requires very expensive maintenance and monitoring systems and very many highly trained personnel for its readiness and operation. By definition, the targets for such systems must be economically justified for such an expense. Missiles cannot be targeted at small villages or farming communities!

The second disadvantage of a nuclear attack is that there is no follow through capability to support the use of the missile weapons system. The radiation half life of a nuclear detonation is so great that the successful adversary cannot claim his prize! In addition, there is not much of prize (city or country) left to claim. The third problem is that any use of the system invites instant response in kind from the enemy. Detection systems preclude any evasive action or practical defensive action so the advantage of surprise with a pre-emptive strike is no longer available. Notwithstanding the doomsday characterization of these modern weapons, experience has demonstrated that all great wars had foolish beginnings and that as long as countries are in an adversarial position, they will either by design or accident eventually collide with each other with the weapons that are available. Based on history all too often disputes between countries have been resolved with the force of arms.

Although there never has been an absolutely fail-safe defense system, the one system that probable offers the best protection is economic. Put in another way, the value of a military target must justify the economic deployment of resources required for the use of the weapons system. Considered in this light the U.S. and Europe offer the most attractive targets with their high density of industrial and urban populations. The far East and the southern hemisphere would seem to provide the least valuable targets. Japan would be the exception to the rule. For the U.S. the obvious solution is to reduce such vulnerability by dispersion of the great population centers of the Northeast, Midwest and the West coast. Although history would suggest that a major city must first be destroyed before remedial action can be taken, it would appear that dispersion of these major population centers has already started because of other technological factors. Dispersion is already underway!

There are also problems with the peaceful use of nuclear energy as well as unlimited opportunities to improve the quality of life for the human race. The biggest problem is the reluctance (refusal) to recognize and work with the limiting and restrictive design parameters imposed by the very nature of the material itself. It cannot be treated and handled in the same manner as coal, fuel oil or any other fossil fuel. It is a new (i.e. new to mankind) form of energy and comes to us with its own natural laws and regulations which must be complied with or its use will be denied along with penalties for the abuse of this new found source of power. These new laws and regulations do not recognize nor are they beholden to any political, economic or military laws or regulations. Nuclear energy has its own ontology independent of any other form of energy and we have the option of becoming its slave or its master.

One of the problems with nuclear power as far as urban centers are concerned is the predilection of the utility companies to locate their power plants as close as possible to the load centers which has been the center of our cities. Notwithstanding the air pollution over the cities from the coal fired plants, these plants continue to operate at their old locations because people are more fearful of replacing them with nuclear power plants. It should be noted that nuclear power plants have been operating in the U.S. for the last forty years and there has not been a single casualty. Even with the old technology nuclear energy boast an unparalleled safety record in the United States. Casualties from air pollution from fossil fuel plants are another matter. One of the difficulties with nuclear power in the U.S. is the failure of the utility companies to utilize qualified people in the operation of the nuclear systems. There are no licensing requirements for the individuals in the plants and the properly licensed professional engineers are too few and far between. This is not only an opportunity for disaster, but very unprofitable as well.

A classic example of the failure to recognize nuclear energy for what it really is and what is required to harness this enormous source of power, is the disaster at Chernobyl in the former Soviet Union. On April 26, 1986 the reactor's core exploded releasing radiation that was nearly 200 times that of the combined releases from the atomic bombs at Hiroshima and Nagasaki. The fire which burned out of control for five days, spewed more than 50 tons of radioactive fallout across Belarus, Ukraine and western Russia. Thousands of villages were abandoned, schools were closed, factories closed and prime cattle slaughtered by the ton. People fled their homes with only the clothes on their back. Yet, this is not the worst industrial accident of modern times. So far, 1996, fewer than 500 people have died as a direct result of the accident. By contrast the chemical leak at Bhopal, India in 1984 killed at least 2,000 people and injured some 200,000. Incidentally, the Chernobyl plant is still in operation. We do not yet know all of the facts about this accident, except that all reports indicate that housekeeping was poor to very bad, security very lax and most importantly, manpower was inept, untrained and lacking any professional engineering supervision or direction. This crude primitive plant staffed by incompetents would not have been permitted in any Western nation. This would have been a formula for disaster even in a coal fired plant with its high pressure boilers, let alone a nuclear reactor.

Since cities have traditionally been the center of social and economic activity, it was only logical that they were also the load center for all regional electrical power and steam consumption. Electrical power plants have used fossil fuels for the generation of electricity for the last 100 years. Coal is by far the most common and most economical fuel used although oil and natural gas make up a substantial amount of the balance with hydro and nuclear power accounting for less than 25% of the total consumption at this time for the country. Power plants have therefore been located as close as possible to the load centers which in turn are very close to the center of most American cities. At the turn of the last century the urban centers included the factories, office buildings, retail centers, hospitals, libraries, schools and public buildings which not only obtained their power from the utility power plants, but in many cases also purchased steam from the same power plants for their central heating systems and/or their indus-

trial processes. In most major cities today these power plants are still function-
ing along with their very elaborate distribution systems of underground electric
power cables and steam tunnels. Along with the very heavy investment in these
power plants and distribution systems, the maintenance and replacement cost of
the equipment and facilities is extremely high. Since most of the demand for
electrical power is in the suburban and rural parts of the country, the utility
companies can operate these systems in the urban centers only by increasing the
prices for power in the rural areas where the demand is greater.
Nuclear power has been severely limited in its growth because of the reluctance
of utility companies to relocate the power centers away from the load centers.
Public opposition to nuclear power is to a considerable extent justified since no
power plant of any kind should be located in a population center. After many
years of ever increasing demand for more electrical power, the products of combustion from fossil fuel fired plants along with automobiles using gasoline, have
now saturated the atmosphere with air pollution that threatens all of our major
urban centers. An increasing number of cities in Europe are also affected with
this problem and on both continents the problem is spreading with alarming
speed.

An obvious remedy for this problem is to substitute nuclear power for fossil
fuels and electric motors for automobile gasoline engines. Nuclear power also
has problems, but better engineering and most importantly, more remote locations for power plants are the best solution for these problems and increased
reductions of carbon dioxide and acid rain in the atmosphere. Utility companies
are loath to abandon their power plants at their present load center locations
because of their heavy investments in these facilities, but with the current trends
in population movements into the rural parts of America, the economics of load
center location could change in the not too distant future if they haven't already.
It would certainly be safer and more comfortable for these plants to be located
away from our major population centers. These locations should be at least 200
miles and preferably 300 miles away from the major urban centers.

One of the most promising advancements in recent years has been the development of a new kind of reactor which practically eliminates the few hazards
that now exist. It is called the HTGR, the "high temperature gas-cooled reactor",

and is currently being pioneered in Germany. One of this reactor's advantages is that it can be made in a factory, where quality control always exceeds that of on-site construction. Another advantage is political. This new reactor uses 20% enriched uranium fission fuel. At no point in its three year fuel cycle can the reactor produce materials for making nuclear weapons. The economics are very promising too. As of 1990 the system was producing power at approximately 5.8 cents per kilowatt hour. The HTGR design may well be the first to over-come both political and environmental objections. According to reports the Audubon Society supports this technology and once they get the facts the public will do the same.

Historically civilizations have developed around sources of energy. The mighty cedars of Lebanon provided fuel as well as naval stores for the Phoeni-cians, Hittites and other ancient cultures. The coal deposits of the Ruhr helped fuel the industrial age for Europe and the coal deposits in England were the mainspring of the industrial revolution in the 18th and 19th century. In the U.S. the coal deposits in Pennsylvania were the basis of one of the greatest industrial expansions in the world in the 19th century. Even though our oil and gas sup-plies now reach out through the most extensive distribution network in the world and coal fuels our power plants in every major urban center because of our extensive railroad systems, the U.S. still has vast areas that are undeveloped because there is no electrical power or water supply. Nuclear power and in particular small package power plants fueled with nuclear energy will solve this problem and make any place on the map attractive for development. Once elec-tric power is economically available water can be piped to any point where it is needed. New towns and urban centers will use nuclear power plants when elec-tric power lines cannot reach their locations economically from existing power plants.

Today, in 1996, any analysis of new towns in rural America or living in our large urban centers must consider the role of international terrorism relative to nuclear energy. In this regard there are two divisions of this uncomfortable subject to be concerned about. The first category might be labeled military or quasi military where a bomb or nuclear device is delivered to a specific target for detonation. The second might be characterized as sabotage where a bomb or nuclear device is planted in a strategic utility and subsequently detonated. In either case, the deeds can only be carried out by an organized effort which has access to all of the necessary resources for such attacks. The acts of the terrorist are different than the acts of an assassin whose target is most always a single individual such as a government official, letter bomb recipient, airplane hijacker, etc.. The terrorist seeks a much larger target including many more victims.

Although terrorism consumes more and more news print and television time these days, it is a problem of increasing dimensions only because most of the governments of the world refuse to acknowledge the true definition of the problem. Terrorism is no more or no less than another dimension of "modern warfare". The purpose of warfare is to bring the adversary population to its knees using any method it can to guarantee success. If the challenger has nuclear weapons available and he can afford to use them, such weapons will be used. If all he can afford are biological or chemical weapons, than these will be used. If all he can afford are small arms and the element of surprise, these will be used. War is war, is war, is war, etc.. The real problem is to accurately identify who you are at war with and the reason that the adversary party chooses war as a remedy for his problem. It would appear that modern governments have not yet followed this rationale in their response to terrorist attacks and can therefore only look forward to more attacks with increasing intensity since like any art form, once the learning curve is accomplished, the production aspects of the task become much more efficient and frequent. There are some key requirements for the success of a terrorist attack that are directly related to urban centers. First, and most important, television coverage is mandatory. Without television the attack is practically worthless as far as political objectives are concerned. Second, the target must be a major urban center or an ancillary to such a center, e.g. an airport, arena or any other high visibility population center. Third, the people carrying out the attack must be expendable, emotionally and/or mentally unstable. Religious zealots, paranoid schizophrenics and other psychotic individuals who use politics to camouflage their behavior are the most common messengers for these attacks. The real conspirators of course are far removed from the scene of the attack. All of these ingredients are all too common and readily available with today's technology and a very unstable society.

In spite of any advertising or government proclamations to the contrary, the American public with the advantage of daily television and newspapers can measure these situations with good accuracy. The defensive reaction is clear. First, don't enter a war zone. If you do you enter at your peril. Second, do not work or live in an economically attractive target area. Simple analysis tells any reasonable person that the target which produces the most successful results for the terrorist is that which is located at the center of the greatest population density. It is only at these points that television coverage is practically guaranteed, e.g. airports, large cities, etc.. To avoid such morbid encounters the remedies are obvious. Avoid travel to war zones at all cost and do not work or live in areas of high population concentrations.

Notwithstanding the differences of the various nations of the western world, they have much more in common then the differences that separate them. Differences between these countries and the third world however, are much greater and there's the rub. Today's third world countries are the "have not" nations, but they do possess all of the technologies of the mass transport, modern television, electronic broadcasting, preventative medicine and most importantly, knowledge of nuclear weapons along with educated leadership. These ingredients combined with the rising expectations of people in the third world make for a turbulent future for the superpowers of the western world.

Under the circumstances what can be done to prevent "portable" nuclear bombs from being hand carried to any point in the United States and detonated? The bomb that destroyed the Federal building in Oklahoma City in 1995 and killed 168 people could easily have been nuclear. Nuclear materials once confined to highly controlled government facilities have made their way to the international black market. It is theoretically possible to make a well designed nuclear bomb from a mass of plutonium the size of a can of beer. A crude nuclear device which requires less expertise, but more fissionable material, could be delivered by a small truck. Even a crude one kiloton nuclear explosion would be hundreds of times more powerful than the Oklahoma blast. Recent reports (1996) indicate that Russian army troops are selling their weapons abroad, often through Mafia middle men. Russian officials have denied that any smuggling has involved weapons grade material, but terrorist aren't that selective. They would be satisfied with lower grade uranium or the kind of plutonium found in spent nuclear reactor fuel rods. So far seven confirmed cases of theft from the former Soviet Union involve such weapons-usable materials, ingredients that could make a nuclear device capable of killing hundreds of thousands of people.

Under our present system of government about the only remedy available to prevent either portable nuclear bombs or those that may be sent with an ICBM from a rogue nation including biological bombs, from being delivered to target areas in the U.S., is to institute martial law at all sensitive target areas, e.g. water supply stations, airports, strategic bridges, sports arenas, churches, subway stations, etc., in other words at all areas of public assembly. It goes without saying that such a remedy is not going to be very popular. The only other remedy to provide maximum assurance and/or protection from such random acts of violence is to make the targets so small that they would not be economically justified. These weapons and their delivery systems are not cheap and to justify their use, that is to attract the most public attention, they can be deployed at only those targets which have the greatest density of population and/or the most severe economic impact. Where it is not possible to achieve such diversification (including residential), martial law must be imposed to provide the required security. This would include of course all of the important bridges, water supply stations, airports, sports arenas, power plants (especially nuclear plants), etc..

Before one dismisses such an undertaking as too draconian or even unworkable in our society consider some of the more recent events following the sad experiences in Oklahoma and the World Trade Center in New York. The cult of Aum Shinrikyo is highly suspect of setting off a nuclear explosion in the Australian outback in 1993. They had also been trying to buy Russian nuclear warheads and had set up an advanced laboratory on their 500,000 acre ranch in Australia where they had been mining uranium, a most important material for making atomic bombs. It should be noted that this Japanese doomsday cult is accused of the poison-gas attack on Tokyo subways in 1995 that killed 12 people and injured thousands. After this attack investigators learned that this secret group, Aum Shinrikyo or Supreme Truth, had accumulated some $1 billion and won over more than 50,000 converts in at least six countries. In all fairness it must be pointed out that authorities are not yet convinced that this explosion in Australia was nuclear in origin. The seismic evidence indicates that the explosion could also have been an earthquake or even a meteor, but some of the other circumstances make the nuclear origin highly suspect.

Along with this troublesome news which was made public on January 23, 1997 in the New York Times, we were also informed that none other than the United States is now selling missile delivery systems (which it once banned) on the world market in open competition with the Russians. Since the French and the British are also in the arms business we might safely assume that they too will be in the market place with their wares so they can keep their employment up in these industries.

And so it would appear that what we are seeing is the same progression with these weapon systems that occurred with the submarine, the machine gun and the aeroplane. Remember, at one time even the crossbow was banned from so called civilized warfare (unless you were trying to kill infidels).

CHAPTER 9

AMERICA'S BIG CITIES

What will happen to the large urban centers in America? For the most part they were created by technology. Now that the technology has changed will the cities also change or will they be abandoned as many cities have been abandoned in ancient times as well as in modern times. Although wars, pestilence, climate changes and natural disasters devastated many cities and towns which never recovered, Carthage, Troy, the ancient Mayan cities, and the thousands of ghost towns in the U.S., the most common cause for failure to survive was the elimination of an economic base for the support of the community.

Large cities in America as we know them today are primarily the result of the industrial revolution of the 19th and 20th century. The obsolescence and decay of many of these cities is based on two categories of technological changes which together made for the creation of new communities and a new life style outside of the older city. As new manufacturing methods and transportation improvements dictated the construction of new factories, old facilities had to be abandoned because of the exorbitant cost of converting the old facilities and the increasing cost of maintaining the supporting infrastructure for these commercial and industrial buildings. The second category of technological change was the development of a more desirable life style or country living which is now available without the toil and inconvenience that burdened our grandparents.

Big cities got that way because commerce and industry spawned by the industrial revolution built their factories, warehouses and offices there. That's where all the supporting resources were located; the mills and factories had to have steam, electric power, rail lines, copious fresh water supplies, sewers, fire protection, police protection and most importantly a large labor supply. The labor supply needed housing, schools, public transportation, hospitals and retail stores. They (labor) also needed libraries, newspapers, churches, police and fire protection and even entertainment which meant a baseball diamond, public park and even a zoo or theatre. None of this was available in the rural countryside before W.W. II. All of this was provided in the big city and American industry took advantage of it. From the turn of the century up to W.W. II factories seemed to beget more factories. At the same time farmers, made redundant by tractors and reapers, and immigrants poured into the cities to work in the factories. By the turn of the century a nation that had been 90% rural twenty five years before was becoming unmistakenly urban. By the end of W.W. I the big cities were well defined and growing. Unlike the major cities of Europe, Asia and South America, America's metropolises were the centers of the manufacturing industry.

It wasn't very long after this that anyone who had a choice wanted to get away from these manufacturing centers, especially if heavy industry was the principal enterprise. No one wanted to live next to a foundry or stamping plant with the heavy air pollution and the incessant noise from the hammers and presses. The problems were exacerbated and went 'round the clock when the plants started two or even three shifts. In the early days zoning either did not exist or did little or nothing to help the home owner. Once the automobile replaced the horse for America's transportation, the labor force including the executives, became mobile; the suburbs were born and the decentralization of the big cities had begun. These trends were well established until the stock market crash of 1929 started the nation's plunge into the Great Depression. By 1931 the auto industry was operating at one-fifth capacity and the steel mills banked their fires in Detroit, Gary and Pittsburgh. The depression was wide spread and hit hard. 25% of the labor force was out of work. Businesses failed, people lost their life savings as the banks closed many of which never opened again. People lost their homes and were evicted by the same banks that had taken their life savings! Suburban development slowed to a halt. The migration to the cities reversed temporarily as many of the unemployed returned to small towns or the farms. All of the governments efforts provided little or no relief from the depression. The economy finally recovered when the government began spending vast sums of money on tanks, guns and planes to fight Hitler and Japan. After ten years of neglect from the depression, the war years increased the wear and tear on the cities and buildings. Unless repairs and or replacements were directly related to the war effort, everything was postponed indefinitely. Housing was especially hard hit since without replacements or additions, the old houses and apartments, most of which were built in the 1920s, had to accommodate the migrants who moved to the urban centers to man the war production plants. In one sixty-one dwelling unit apartment building in Detroit, Michigan there were one hundred and eighty families living with three to six members per family!

The depression years of the 30s followed by the war years of the 40s took a heavy toll of the cities' infrastructure, buildings and equipment. Very few buildings or utilities were built during this period and the wear and tear on the old facilities during these times of great social and economic upheaval was exacerbated by the anachronistic tax systems and just plain neglect. By the end of W.W. II the offices, manufacturing plants and the housing facilities were not only worn out for the most part, but they were now obsolete as well! Houses had inadequate wiring and insufficient electrical power for the new appliances and lighting loads; manufacturing buildings constructed to carry enormous floor loads had only 16 foot clearances between massive columns and ceiling clearances of only 8 or 10 feet. Once the electrical cable trays and bus duct were hung from the ceiling, there was no room for the plumbing lines, new lighting fixtures, or the fire protection sprinkler lines. Modern manufacturing equipment and methods needed 40 to 50 foot clearances between columns and 12 to 25 foot vertical clearances. In addition, new plumbing and fire protection codes could not be met in the old buildings and 19th century sewers could not carry the waste from the factories or the housing units without discharging the excessive flows directly into the rivers and lakes without any treatment. Added to this condition was the very poor state of support facilities (infrastructure), e.g. streets, bridges, sewers, steam tunnels and water supply lines which not only could not carry the traffic and hydraulic loads, but had suffered from neglect and in many cases downright abuse, during the war years.

In the years immediately following the war the first signs of growth and
expansion appeared in the suburbs, i.e. the small communities adjoining the
large urban centers. The popularity and success of these first major commercial
developments was unprecedented. The modern retail store which moved to the
shopping mall in the suburbs quickly changed America's buying habits and the
movement away from the urban center began in full force. By the mid 1960s not
only were the new and elegant shopping malls in practically all of the major
suburbs of America, but the secondary or strip shopping centers began to appear
throughout the rural countryside. One of the most powerful and pervasive transportation improvements for urban, suburban and rural development was the
Interstate Freeway system. Once these freeways were completed the advantage
of a central business and commercial district disappeared. Any location on a
freeway was just as accessible as anywhere else and most importantly, free
parking was available! For some strange reason most all big cities look on parking as a source of revenue and ignore the frustration and discouragement such a
system engenders. By the mid 60s all of the large cities were encircled by giant
shopping malls with free parking and the smaller strip malls dotted the countryside with their offers of goods and services for the entire country. Very soon
developers began building office buildings near the malls and the trickle of
corporate relocations became a flood. By the 1970s the suburbs surpassed the
big cities in employment. The high rise office buildings in Washington's suburbs in Virginia and Maryland now contain more office space than the District
itself.

Manufacturing had started to abandon the mill towns and the big cities in
the 60s and relocate to the cornfields of rural America closer to their market
centers and their labor supply. All of the resources needed to operate modern
manufacturing plants were now available in the rural countryside! The logistical
requirements for locating a new heavy manufacturing plant are expensive and
very often complex. Electric power is one of the more important requirements
and since the Rural Electric Administration began electrifying rural America in
1934, all but the most remote wilderness areas in the country have unlimited
power available for any industry. Good transportation is high on the priority list
for any manufacturing facility. A mobile labor force must have good access to

the plant. Materials must be received without excessive shipping penalties and finished products must be shipped to customers. Good access to the interstate freeway system along with economical approaches to main rail lines is an absolute requirement for every new plant site location. For many industries access to airports and shipping docks is also essential. Potable water supplies and provision for waste treatment facilities must also be available. There are many other requirements, reasonable land prices, equitable taxes, good soil conditions, proper zoning, stable conditions in earthquake regions, etc., but for all of these probably the most important today is an adequate and well educated labor supply. At this time these essential requirements are most often satisfied by locating the new industrial complex in the rural country side. Without substantial government subsidies to remove the old and obsolete facilities in the big cities, the older large urban centers cannot provide these new plant sites and meet these requirements for modern industry.

The combination of commercial development, manufacturing industries and shopping malls moving to the suburbs, have now formed the cornerstone of the 21st century metropolis! It would seem that Thomas Jefferson had the vision and foresight to see how our citizens and their country should be developed. He said, "cultivators of the earth are the most valuable citizens" and government could be virtuous only as long as there shall be vacant lands." Urban workers, merchants, financiers, all are sources of corruption when "piled up upon one another" in "pestilential cities," which he considered "sores" on the body politic. Jefferson didn't trust the cities. He believed in a nation of small farmers living near self-contained villages. When he drafted the plan to organize the Northwest Territories with the Northwest Ordinance of 1787, he visualized an American countryside made up of a logical grid of self-sufficient communities. Although he believed America would be happiest if it remained primarily a rural nation, he admitted in his later years that industrialism was necessary to give the country an independent economy. Jefferson's most important goal was to give individual men a wider liberty. It looks like this vision may come true in the 21st century with manufacturing replacing agriculture as the economic base for the country.

In the 1920s and the 1930s after W.W. I when people were moving to their
new homes from the farm to the city, two of the outstanding benefits were
indoor plumbing with flush toilets and electric lights. In this same time period
with the advent of the radio and the electric refrigerator, the gap between living
in the country with oil lamps, wood burning cook stoves, outdoor manual pumps
for fresh water and outhouses 50 to 100 feet from the house, and living in the
city, was more pronounced than ever. The city slicker, even if he lived in a
slum, was so much better off than the farmer that little or no thought was given
to returning to the country to become a "hick" farmer. Technology soon
changed this picture. In 1934 the federal government launched the Rural
Electrification Administration (REA) which would soon bring electricity to all
of rural America. With electricity water could be brought to the house under
pressure and the manual hand pump could become a relic. Water under pressure
could activate the flush toilets and with the development of the septic tank the
complete plumbing system could now be installed that would be comparable to
anything in the city. Electricity also brought in the radio and the telephone
which meant that the long lonely nights could be filled with entertainment and
gossip to make the farm living room every bit as modern as any house in the
city.

In 1934 the FHA was also started by the federal government in a weak
attempt to help people own their own homes. Since loans were limited to 1/3 to
1/2 the value of the house, the program wasn't very effective. By 1950 after
W.W. II the housing shortage was so bad that FHA changed its down payment
requirements to 10% of the house value and with the drop in interest rates,
housing production increased dramatically. Thousands of families could now
afford a house. Practically none of these houses were built in the big cities.
There was no vacant land for the new houses and the cost of demolition and
land development in an old city was prohibitive. What is not generally
understood is that the practice in the construction trades is for the demolition
contractor to remove the old building structures down to the grade (ground)
level only. All of the underground structures, e.g. foundations, basements,
sewers, gas lines, steam tunnels, electrical conduits, etc., must be removed with
heavy excavation equipment which is another trade as distinct from demolition.

But what really exacerbated the housing problem for the cities were the thousands of vacant scattered lots that were only 16 or 20 feet wide and therefore could not meet the new standards of FHA for minimum lot sizes. To correct this problem old plats would have had to be abandoned and new plats created with the proper lot sizes. This was an almost incorrigible problem since many existing houses were on the old platted lots.

The suburbs were soon filled to overflowing with new FHA subdivision and many of these new developments reached into the Townships of rural America. VA loan insurance had been added in 1944 and added to the money flowing into housing. Housing starts jumped from 114,000 in 1944 to 1,696,000 in 1950, but few if any were in the big cities. Since buying a new house was often cheaper than renting and the interest on mortgage payments was income tax deductible, the percentage of American families who owned houses increased from 44% in 1940 to 68% in 1972. Most of the land in the suburbs adjoining the big cities has long since been filled with housing. Today practically all of the new housing subdivisions are being developed in the townships and counties of unincorporated parts of America!

Why didn't the older and larger urban centers respond to the challenge and meet the needs and desires of an expanding population? The most direct answer to this question is that the management and leadership of these communities failed to adequately comprehend the impact of a growing and rapidly changing technological culture coupled with an unprecedented demand for better living standards. The cities and their industries that mobilized for the war effort of W.W. II were designed and built during the 1920s and the very early 1930s. With the Great Depression of the 1930s few if any new manufacturing plants, commercial buildings or housing developments were built. All that happened in the war years was the accelerated use, abuse and depreciation of the basic infrastructure in the cities with practically no accommodation to modern equipment, vehicles, housing or manufacturing processes. Thousands of single family homes for example were built between 1910 and 1930 with no provision for automobile storage. Many do not even have driveways for access to the back yard. Most all of the housing including multi-family apartments are built on lots that are serviced by back alleys. The original concept of an alley was to provide

convenient access for garbage and trash collection as well as a location for telephone and electric power poles and lines servicing the houses so that the front
yards and house elevations would look attractive. Keeping the alleys clean and
with reasonable snow removal became such a massive problem that most cities
have long since abandoned the effort. Industry faced comparable problems with
their facilities. Zoning boundaries and requirements along with obsolete building codes were made up before the turn of the century. These restrictions now
limited industrial plant expansion and more importantly set industry up as targets for litigation by their residential neighbors for air, and water pollution
along with traffic and noise problems.

Property taxing policies then exacerbated the problem for both industry and
housing. If a resident fixed up his front porch and painted his house, the asses-
sor increased his taxes. If a manufacturing plant paved their parking lot or added
a transformer to increase the electrical power for the plant, his taxes were also
increased. Most importantly nothing was done by the cities to encourage the
construction or the maintenance of housing or industrial facilities. In fact major
improvements needed to keep pace with competition were almost always financed by the industries themselves in spite of the heavy tax burdens. Com-
pounding the problems for housing and industry was the accelerated decay of
the urban infrastructure. Hailed by some as the "Urban Apocalypse", the aging
and neglected network of the nations streets, roads, bridges, water supply facilities, sewers, dams and rails are held together by prayers and promises. These are
"Public Works" and not only housing and industry, but agriculture depend on
public works for their growth and expansion let alone survival. Nationally the
country would have to spend up to $3 trillion just to maintain today's level of
service on public facilities according to some experts. Most cities and states
have just thrown up their hands at such estimates, but meantime the problems
get worse. In Jersey City, N.J. in 1982 the water supply ran out when an 82 year
old main broke in mid summer leaving 223,000 residents without water or fire
protection. It took five days to restore drinkable water. In Colorado in the same
month 80 year old Lawn Lake Dam gave way sending 250 million gallons of
water through the resort town of Estes Park. Four people were killed and damage ran to $21 million. As John Wiedeman, former president of the American

Society of Civil Engineers put it: "Virtually every part of the country has its own horror story." Some 8,000 miles of the recently completed 42,944 mile interstate freeway system, started in the 1950s, are crumbling and must be resurfaced. Nearly 45% of the nation's 557,516 bridges are classified as "either structurally deficient or obsolete." Of the total of officially "deficient bridges," 126,655 are so unsafe as to be restricted by law to light vehicles or closed to traffic altogether. At least 3,416 bridges have been closed for repairs or for good. The Transportation Department estimates the cost of replacing or rehabilitating all bridges at $47.6 billion. To repair the 8,000 miles of the interstate-highway system would require $952 billion according to the department. Leakage from an aging water distribution system cost New York, Boston, Buffalo and other cities as much as one third of their water supplies. Pumps must work continuously around the clock to keep this same water from flooding the New York subway system. Similar stories abound for the nations sewers and waste treatment plants serving all of the urban centers.

    Why did local, state and federal authorities allow these important facilities to deteriorate to these poor conditions? First there is the common perception that public works as well as other building structures, e.g. houses, schools, office buildings, churches, etc., never wear out! In a profit oriented culture it is difficult to invest in maintenance of facilities that "appear" to never wear out. The pyramids in Egypt have been up for 5,000 years, some of the cathedrals in Europe have been up and are still being used, for hundreds of years and even the most famous road built by the Romans 2,000 years ago, the Appian Way, is still in existence; so why shouldn't all buildings and public works last forever? Few people would question the need to change the oil for an automobile or to replace the tires, but as we know all too well, buildings and especially the structures that are not seen every day, e.g. water mains, sewers, etc. are the last to be budgeted and all too often postponed to next years budget. Whatever the reasons, the problems are now so massive and widespread that it will probable take a program not unlike the public works programs in the 1930s during the depression, to repair the entire infrastructure and prevent the collapse of the nation's economy.

However, it is dangerous to compare today's buildings and public works with the structures of antiquity. It should be remembered that there were thousands of these structures in ancient times and practically all of them are long gone. The magnificent Roman highway system with all of its bridges, port facilities and public water supply aqueducts and reservoirs, quickly disappeared when they were no longer maintained and most of the pyramids in Egypt are to this day covered with sand and not even accessible without a great deal of archaeological money and effort. In fact, buildings, utilities, water lines, sewers, roads and bridges must be maintained to continue to give service and even with good maintenance they do wear out and have to be replaced. Another important factor is "obsolescence". Many facilities even though they are still in good condition are useless because of obsolescence. The old combined sewer systems in Detroit that serve over four million people continue to pollute the Detroit river and should have been replaced decades ago. Note, combined sewers with sanitary and storm flow in the same sewer pipe are no longer permitted, but the hundreds of miles of old sewers have not been replaced with separate sewers. Narrow two and three lane highways are very unsafe, but continue to be used because the pavements are still in good condition. Many bridges are still in good condition for the highway loads of fifty years ago, but are very unsafe with today's truck loads. Obsolescence is a major problem in today's older urban centers.

As we have seen our major urban centers struggle with the burden of worn out and obsolete public works it would be worthwhile to consider the fate of other cities that have not survived before massive subsidies of public money are spent trying to revitalize these dinosaurs. The history of the ghost towns of Michigan, Colorado, Nevada, California and the northwest gives us some indication of what to expect. Colorado has approximately 2,000 ghost towns first built and then abandoned as a result of the great gold rush days of the 19th century. As soon as the "color" (gold) played out, the town was abandoned. Leadville and Cripple Creek, Colorado were typical which in the mining heydays of the 1890s had populations in excess of 5,000. The town of Cripple Creek was founded by D.C. Williams who opened a boarding house in a tent; a saloon, consisting of a plank over two beer barrels, and a dirt road. By 1893 the town had eight lumber yards, twenty six saloons, ten meat markets, nine hotels, forty four lawyers' offices and thirty six real estate offices. Leadville and many other Colorado towns had a similar beginning. Today, these small communities are tourist attractions during the summer months except for Vale and Aspen which have become a major ski resorts. Many towns in America's farm belt which were created for the most part by the railroads, have been abandoned just in recent years since W.W. II. Kansas alone has 2,000 ghost towns, and countless other towns that haven't attracted some manufacturing or service industry are rapidly disappearing.

Roy L. Dodge's excellent three volume catalog list over a thousand Michigan ghost towns. Most of them are gone without a trace. Hundreds more range from lonesome sites where almost nothing is left to mark their former existence, to others where only a few crumbling houses and buildings remain. In some, people are still living there, but they are only a shadow of what they once were. Mining for copper and iron ore in the Upper Peninsula fostered many of these towns and as all of Michigan was the leader in the nation in lumber production from 1870 through the turn of the century, hundreds of "instant" towns were created to support this tremendous industry with saw mills, rail heads, hotels, stores, saloons, churches, blacksmith shops and everything else needed for the equipment and housing of the labor force needed to clear the forest and get the timber to market. Once the white pine timbers were located and cut they were moved to the nearest waterway which eventually led to one of the lumber ports on the Great Lakes; Bay City, Detroit, Alpena, Muskegon or Traverse City. From these port cities the schooners moved across the lakes to the Erie Canal and then to the world. Except for some of the larger towns, Detroit, Grand Rapids, or Bay city, many of these Michigan towns have disappeared altogether, but some survive to this day as tourist centers or even manufacturing centers, but few ever reached the population heights that they enjoyed in the heyday of the lumber industry.

A typical town was McKinley, Michigan located in the northern part of the lower peninsula. The town started in 1884 when a man called Potts purchased the lumbering rights and began cutting timber in the Au Sable River valley. The town grew with the usual additions of drug stores, schools, churches, dance halls, and eleven saloons! A railroad was built to connect the town to the port city of Oscoda on Lake Huron and the town boomed. In 1893 the town name was changed from Potts to McKinley in honor of the president. After a great fire ravaged the town the company moved its operations to Oscoda since most of the timber had been cut out of the McKinley area anyhow. When this happened 2,000 people left the town for employment elsewhere. The town shrank to two houses and did not start to revive until 1940 when electricity and the telephone were brought to the town. Today the town has a bar, small general store and a motel which are all supported by the hunters, fishermen and a few retirees.

Sharon, Michigan is another such town. Originally called "Jam One" because of the enormous log jam created there in the spring of 1870 on the Manistee River. The Post Office rejected that name and the name Sharon was adopted because it sounded so pleasant and peaceful. In addition to the timber industry the town also became an important railroad junction in the 1890s and by 1894 Sharon had became a boomtown of almost two thousand people with a vibrant business district and six lumber mills. At one time there were twelve lumber camps in the area and Sharon or Jam One was anything but a quiet and/or pleasant town. It was the main watering hole for all of the lumberjacks in the area. The legendary Silver Jack Driscol and another lumberjack once fought bare knuckle for one hour and forty five minutes in Peterson's saloon. Peaceful indeed. When the timber finally ran out and the railroads died, Sharon came to its end and finally lost its post office in 1921. Now nothing remains except an old abandoned schoolhouse.

Another good example of the importance of an economic base for an urban center is the case of Houghton County, Michigan. Even before the great gold rush of 1849 Houghton County was the center of the Great Copper rush of 1844. Note, from the Civil War to the turn of the century Michigan produced 70% of the nations copper with Calumet producing more than one half of the state's total. The population of the county grew from 9,000 in 1860 to almost 90,000 by 1910. The county had 10 trains a day going to and from cities like Milwaukee, Chicago and Detroit. It had 20 newspapers in four languages, seven theaters, two opera houses, and street cars running every fifteen minutes. They also had 30 churches, 30 schools and 60 bars! Copper mining has all but disappeared from Michigan and the population of Houghton today is about one third of its former self.

In all of these towns the most significant common denominator was the loss of the economic base. They had all flourished for a while, then languished and died when the timber was gone and/or the ore ran out and the railroad stopped running. Once the mines or the timber were played out there was no more money coming into the town from the outside to support the stores, saloon, hotels, blacksmiths, etc. The economic base is an essential requirement and a fact of life for any town. If it disappears from the town for any reason, the rest of the town, the supper market, hotels, restaurants, retail stores, libraries, schools, hospitals, etc. cannot survive without outside subsidies. These facilities cannot survive by themselves; they derive their life blood from the economic base in the community. Today we are witnessing the creation of new "ghost" towns as the agricultural towns in the Midwest created for the most part by the railroads in the 19th century are being bypassed or ignored by the change in the industry with the loss of government agricultural supports and the change in farming practices leaves these towns with no money to support them. Small farms which were the lifeblood of these towns have been replaced by large conglomerates that do not spend money in the town. Once again the only thing that is constant is change.

A perfect example of a large urban center that lost its economic base is the city of Detroit, Michigan. Originally a trading center established by the French in 1701 on the banks of the Detroit River, it began its real growth after the Erie Canal was completed in 1825. When the railroads with the age of steam began their great expansion in the middle of the 19th century, Detroit was building box cars and stoves. It even assumed the name of the stove capital of America. But it was the automobile that really put Detroit on the map. When Henry Ford started the moving assembly line in his Highland Park plant in 1913 so he could build a car for the average American, Detroit quickly became the automobile capital of the world. No longer a luxury toy for the wealthy, the automobile was now a "necessity" for the general population. It should be noted that Highland Park, today an enclave of Detroit, was then way out in the suburbs of the big city and not long after Ford was building his Model T's and Model A's in Highland Park,

General Motors built their world headquarters on the outskirts of the city, far away from the urban center. General Motors built their factories far away from the high tax locations near the urban centers. Ford soon followed suit by relocating their main manufacturing operations from Highland Park to the then rural location of Dearborn, Henry Ford's birthplace. With these huge automotive operations came thousands of smaller supporting manufacturing operations that located in or near the city of Detroit. Machine tools, stampings, wood products, fabrics, electrical supplies, fuel supplies, warehouses, railheads and marshalling yards, etc., all located as close as possible to their customer for the supply and distribution of their products. After W.W. II this began to change. The city had grown so big that it now embraced all of the smaller enclaves and the thousands of smaller factories that had been located on the outskirts of the original urban center. All of these industries which made up the powerful economic base for the city began to leave for greener pastures where the taxes were not so punitive and most importantly, where there was room to expand. By this time the labor force was so mobile with the very product they were building, that a new plant or office could be located practically anywhere. And so it came to past, the technology that had created the great urban center, had now dismantled it by shifting the economic base from its center to the rural countryside. Today, although the car builders have rebuilt a few of their assembly plants in the city, the vast bulk of the industry is gone and most of the city exist because of government subsidies for the population of one million that remain. If trends of the past are repeated, most of these will leave for more attractive employment opportunities.

The second and perhaps the most important reason for the decay of the large urban centers in America is the failure of the private enterprise system to provide good homes for the urban poor and the failure of this system to use urban and suburban land sensibly and economically. In both cases the failures have occurred because of the anachronistic tax policies including Federal and State as well as local taxes. These tax policies actually rig the profit motive backward when it comes to land use, land development or redevelopment. Unfortunately, taxes all too often direct and dominate real estate decisions. In the first place the system taxes unimproved or under-improved property so lightly that land owners are under no pressure to sell until they are offered many times what their land is worth. The price of the land is established as the capitalized difference between the rent that the land can be expected to earn and the taxes it must be expected to pay. With taxes so low, the price of the land increases to much more than it is really worth. As land prices increase only high rise structures with many more dwelling units can be justified for the expensive land investment. And high rise building cost are at least 50% more expensive per square foot than low rise or single story structures. High construction cost therefore compound the high cost of land. It should also be noted that a great deal, if not all, of the soft cost of such a project, e.g. architectural fees, legal fees, marketing and especially mortgage financing, are a percentage of the hard cost of land and construction.

Along with the counterproductive taxing system on land is the manner in which improvements are taxed. The system taxes improvements so heavily that it makes slums and worn out factories one of the most profitable of all real estate investments. In too many cases it just doesn't pay to improve the property. So the slums are still spreading faster than any urban redevelopment program can clear them out. As few assessors realize if a one or one and one half percent tax on improvements is imposed, it works out to be like paying a 30% completion tax on the installment plan. A 30% tax is a tremendous deterrent to any expenditure. Most importantly, no amount of code enforcement or zoning restrictions will ever keep up with slum formation until the profit is removed from slums by taxation. In the early part of this century land carried nearly half of the national, state and local tax load. That was before the income tax, the inheritance tax, the corporation tax and most of the other nuisance taxes that have since been added. Today, land, which is one third of our national wealth, carries less than 5% of the total tax load. The owners of the slums and idle land are the beneficiaries of such undertaxation. In discussing tax systems that work to the detriment of the city we must also mention rent controls which are imposed from time to time to literally subsidize low income housing. Such a euphemism is just disguising another property tax at the expense of the best and most economical use of the property. Even in times of national emergency rent controls rarely work, but to keep such measures in force in peacetime is actually counter-productive and contributes in no small way to urban decay.

Why should more billions of dollars of tax dollars be put into public hous-ing and urban redevelopment without first finding out if the job can get done better and faster by private enterprise with the profit motive working forward instead of backward. That is by untaxing the improvements which are now over taxed, and shifting the local tax burden to the location values that are under-taxed? This is not just theory. It has worked in practice. In Brisbane, Australia the law since 1896 has forbidden any taxes on improvements, but the unim-proved value of the land is subject to an ad valorem tax (9%) whether you build a fifty story building on it or make it into a parking lot. Some people say this is the only great city in the world without a slum!

The urban blight problem is also compounded by our outdated laws on personal property. In Michigan, as well as many other states, the laws and regu-lations attending the removal of abandoned or junk cars are so horrendous that few if any are ever removed from private property and those left on the street may sit there one to three years before they are removed. As far as cost are con-cerned a minor addition to the annual weight tax would cover all cost for the removal and disposal of abandoned automobiles. It is the legal requirements that are the most formidable obstacle to overcome.

One of the most severe restrictions to progress for our urban centers are the hidebound practices of the trade unions. These requirements imposed by the trades on so many of the essential functions of a city, e.g. police and fire depart-ments, trash collections, rapid transit, public power and lighting, social services, etc., have reached the point of being absurd for most of the large urban centers. Detroit now (1996) pays its trash collectors more money than it does its teach-ers. The pension fund payments for the transit workers by the city of New York nearly bankrupted the city and with the featherbedding that rivals the railroad unions keeps the city on the verge of bankruptcy every year. Although it is ille-gal for public services to strike in most of the states, they strike anyhow and impose such hardship on the community that the cities capitulate rather than fight and then face bankruptcy or higher taxes. Many of the residents then vote with their feet and abandon the city. If a city wants to remain viable and grow it must change all of its union contracts and the way it does business with the unions. No city can tolerate a strike any more than a strike could be tolerated in the army or the navy.

Of all the changes that a city must make to remain viable none is more important than finding a solution to the problem of parking automobiles. Solutions to this problem are not as difficult as it might seem at first glance. Private passenger automobiles must be prohibited in the urban center. Cars must be parked on the city perimeter. Freeways may still be used through the city for emergency vehicles, public transit, commercial carriers and transients. Most importantly, parking on the perimeter must be free! Or at such low cost as to be practically free. Note, this is the case at most all of the airports in the country. To accomplish this, non profit parking lots must be located at strategic locations in or preferably on the periphery of the city. Comfortable and convenient public transit must then be available to move the commuters to the manufacturing, business , commercial or residential parts of the city. Incidentally, and of no small importance, this arrangement would also solve the air pollution problem. In this arrangement all streets would remain as they are to accommodate the handicapped, maintenance, police, fire and other emergency vehicles. Along with these arrangements, commercial and industrial trucks must be allowed to travel designated routes to satisfy the transportation needs of the industrial and commercial centers in the city. The only other option that might be considered is to allow those private passenger cars to use the streets at certain hours for an annual fee of one or two thousand dollars as long as there was no additional air pollution. Obviously the configuration of the city would have to be redesigned and rezoned to make this plan workable. The city could then function as it was supposed to function without the problem of automotive constipation.

The city must replace its economic base if it is to be viable and avoid extinction. To accomplish this goal the city must make itself more attractive than the rural countryside. To become an attractive suitor it must accommodate the needs of industry, commerce or business. Industry must have uncluttered space, good transportation including modern railroad service, adequate electric power, good water supply and sewer service, and most importantly, a very attractive tax incentive.

Does all of this suggest that the large urban centers of today will become ghost towns if they do not meet the new requirements of industry and commerce? Not necessarily, but a distinct possibility. If the economic base of these cities is dwindling or gone altogether the future can not be viable. If the big cities do not make the required changes they will join ancient Thebes, Troy, Babylon, Cripple Creek or McKinley as a page of history. Most importantly the cities must recognize that there will be change. Nothing on this planet remains static or immutable. Longing for the "good 'ole days" or priming the pump with government subsidies will not create new economic basis to support the stores, restaurants, banks, theatres, etc.. Another fact that should be recognized by the urban centers is that "they are no longer needed by the rest of society"! Once you consume more than you contribute, you (or any city) become like a barnacle on the hull of the ship, a parasite. The urban center to survive must make itself needed, if not indispensable to the rest of community.

To make itself "needed" by the rest of the community the urban center must first recognize its true position in the over all plan of the metropolitan family of which it is an integral part. Actually old cities, or urban centers today along with their immediate neighbors, the suburbs, function together as a confederation of independent political units. Many essential municipal operations have been combined or confederated for some time, e.g. water supplies and sewer service, bus service and rapid transit, police and fire protection and of course freeways to mention a few. Essential public utilities such as electric power and telephone, also operate on a regional basis serving the entire metropolitan area. Electric power plants, unit sub stations as well as pumping stations and storage reservoirs are located where they can operate most efficiently, not according to political boundaries. A major part of the problem for the communities in the metropolitan area is that they all try to make believe that they are independent units, but in fact they are not. All of their essential functions are all integrated with each other and any individual community cannot function alone by itself. Only the political and school systems remain unique and independent for content, taxes and financial control.

Technology has been the driving force that has linked these communities together. A major political overhaul of these metropolitan technical confederations would be a quantum leap forward in the revival of the inner cities and the economic efficiency of all of the contiguous suburbs. Home rule constitutional provisions notwithstanding, all of the individual independent political towns in a given metropolitan area are a major impediment to any expansion improvement or addition of a viable economic base for the area. If society cannot resolve this political conundrum then the urban centers, especially the inner cities, will continue to decay and recede to the figure of their former selves, e.g. an agricultural or bucolic park.

Urban change is also severely restricted by the rigid subdivision control laws which prescribe the boundaries of all of the real property in the city and by definition form the basic framework for the property taxes and identification of all of the utilities in the city. Although these laws, the Plat Acts, corrected many of the abuses in land development, they have proven to be almost totally inflexible to cope with changing conditions on the urban scene. True, any legally constituted public agency or agencies which authorized the plat in the first place may also authorize the abandonment of the same plat, but the procedures are so cumbersome and expensive that properly recorded plats are rarely if ever abandoned. New legislation and procedures will be required to mitigate this problem and make the redevelopment of platted land easier and more economical. Twenty and thirty foot lots are just too incompatible with today's housing needs and residential or commercial development.

The zoning of many older urban centers is also in need of review and in many cases revision to meet the requirements of future development and new technology. Much of this effort should be done in conjunction with the revision of property tax laws so well planned zoning will not militate against property tax programs established to encourage new development. It is especially important to provide zoning that will produce a "balanced" community with residential, commercial, institutional and industrial parts of the city arranged to provide the most comfortable living neighborhoods and encourage the maximum investment for commercial and industrial growth. Too many urban centers are unbalanced with unreasonable tax loads on residents or businesses because of the lack of adequate industrial support for the rest of the community.

Just as we experienced the agricultural revolution which was followed by the industrial revolution, we are now told that we are experiencing the third wave or the revolution created by the "information age". Cities as well as all other aspects of life were changed by the first two revolutions, but the jury is still out for us to know to what extent the information age will affect our lives and the future of our cities. Technology was the engine that drove the agricultural and the industrial revolutions and it is again technology that is driving the "information age", but it remains to be seen if the cornucopia that was produced by agricultural and industry can be continued and expanded by the computers and data processors of the new age of information. Although there has been a great deal of hyperbole generated with the new computer technology made available on a mass production scale because of the invention of the micro chip, productivity in the U.S. has not improved very much in recent years and there have been many job and career dislocations resulting from the use of this new technology.

Productivity is that ubiquitous measurement of the amount, valued in dollars, that a worker produces in a given hour, using computers, machinery, knowledge, telecommunication equipment, or a hammer, wrench, tractor, plow or one's head and hands, working alone or with a team at home, in a store, office or factory. This measurement along with other economic indicators, e.g. number of housing starts, number of unemployed and number of employed, number of automobiles, refrigerators, TVs, etc. is some indication of the standard of living we are enjoying and how much the country is growing. Productivity is a direct product of technology and man's ingenuity. With no productivity or with very poor productivity, our standard of living does not improve and in fact it may well evaporate. If productivity is too low the production of goods and services is so inefficient that the cost of these same goods and services becomes so great that the majority of the population cannot afford to purchase them. The automobile is a classic case in point. Until Henry Ford employed Eli Whitney's principle of mass production to building cars, only the rich could afford an automobile.

There is a widespread school of thought today that insist that we have too much technology, that we should eschew any advance work or research on nuclear power, space research, new manufacturing methods, biological changes, genetic engineering, disease control or any effort that will improve the standard of living for ourselves and the rest of the world. The archaeologist are now able to tell us that is just what happened to many of the ancient cities and their people, i.e. productivity declined (for various reasons) and the cities with their civilizations perished. If the cities and the people are to remain viable then productivity must continue and increase with each generation.

From 1870 to 1940 productivity in the U.S. did not improve much notwithstanding all of the inventions and discoveries that took place in that time. Although technology had delivered many improvements that heretofore had not even been dreamed of, the new techniques and machines were not readily incorporated into the mainstream of agriculture, commerce or industry. Consequently the bulk of the population did not reap the benefits of these new ideas and conveniences. This seventy year hiatus was also burdened with one of the worst economic depressions in history. As noted many changes took place with the urban scene, but for the bulk of the population improvements were slow in coming. Thousands of new towns were created and then abandoned in this period and the large urban centers reached population densities in excess of all reasonable limits.

Productivity changed dramatically in 1940. As the U.S. mobilized for the war in Europe every bit of technology that was available was put to the task of increasing production. Machines and men were combined in the most efficient production machines ever created. After a slight dip in 1945 at the end of the war, productivity again increased with major increases in the Gross National Product. Productivity increased two hundred and sixty two percent in the period from 1940 to 1990. No time in the history of the world has so much been produced with so few people. All of this meant more jobs and a higher standard of living for almost everyone. With these increased standards mobility of the labor force increased much to the detriment of the large cities.

Many people have difficulty understanding the concept of an "economic base" for a city. An economic base is that economic activity that brings money into the city from outside of the city. This money is different from the money that changes hands within the city. An example of an economic base in a city is the factory in the city that manufactures refrigerators which are delivered and sold to the rest of the country outside of the city. The proceeds from these sales can then pay the taxes, the wages, the profits and the cost of services to keep the factory in business, e.g. utility bills, repairs, office supplies and of course materials to build the refrigerators. Money that merely changes hands within the city would be retail sales, e.g. clothing, groceries, restaurants, gas stations, etc., hotel accommodations, entertainment and landscaping services to mention a few.

One of the best examples of a large urban center that has a very strong economic base is New York City. Although most all of the large urban centers in the world are the composites of many ancient cultures superimposed on each other, New York is of relatively recent origin and undoubtedly represents the ultimate in technological achievements for the nineteenth and twentieth century. Included with this mass of technological changes that have taken place in the last 150 years are without a doubt some of the greatest number of anthropological and cultural conflicts and paradoxes that have ever been experienced in history. What is amazing is that notwithstanding the conflicts and frustrations from all of these encounters, the system still works!

Although New York continues its obtuse growth in spite of its many physical problems, the reason the city remains viable appears in sharp contrast to the trends in most other American urban centers. Whereas most of the large urban centers in America are no longer needed or desired by the vast majority of the population, the pendulum of public sentiment has not yet moved as far in that direction for New York and possibly Chicago and San Francisco. In these great urban centers there is still the need for American commerce and the desire for the fruits of Western culture to motivate and continue their expansion. For an economic base, New York City is the financial capital of the world and the major financial institutions which service most of the American economy are headquartered there. In addition, practically every country in the world has a branch bank in New York. There are an estimated four hundred foreign and domestic banks in New York City.

Also important is the fact that the city is still the mecca of Western culture for the arts, literature and the telecommunications industry. Such important features of our life style as the entertainment industry, the publishing and television industries are not only headquartered in New York, but the city is also the main center of their operations and the source of their talent. In addition, the more sophisticated art forms such as the opera, classical music, legitimate theatre and the brokerage of classical and modern oil paintings all call New York their home for composition, business operations and performances. It is no coincidence that these industries and institutions are also close to the large financial institutions.

Add to these outstanding focal points of American culture the center of international political exchange, the United Nations, along with the center of trading for American capital, the New York Stock Exchange, the largest port of entry to the U.S., and perhaps the largest international system of airports in the world and we find a city that is not only very much needed by the American economy, but also a very attractive place to live for a great many people. Textile manufacturing is no longer as big an industry in the city that it once was, but the fashion industry still calls New York home and some of the largest retail stores in the country are in New York. Even though the city faces many serious physical and social problems, it still possesses those most important ingredients that make a city viable and "oriented" for growth, namely, it is needed and it is desired by the rest of the country. As a result the money flows into the economic bases of the city which can then support all the other services which make up the city.

It is important to recognize however, that although these important ingredients still prevail in New York, the pendulum has begun to swing in the opposite direction for this city too and without good management along with some draconian measures needed to correct some of the problems, the negative trends will increase and intensify as it has in other American cities. The physical plant for the city, the so called infra structure, has depreciated almost to the point of no return in many cases and the cost of maintenance and repairs now exceeds the ability of the revenue systems to correct the problems. Recent studies for example show that the losses of water in the water distribution system from leakage now equals the amount of daily consumption in the city (New York). Similar conditions exist for the streets, sewer systems, steam tunnels, subway tunnels, electrical conduits, etc. along with the docks, hospitals, jails, schools and parks.

Money is of course the major problem. It would appear that the tax rates have already passed the point of diminishing returns. When an attempt was made a few years ago to increase taxes for the securities industry, the entire industry almost left the city. The effort was quickly rescinded. City taxes are 9% and state taxes 10% , circa 1985, on business profits! These rates are probably the highest in the country and in any event do not encourage capital expansion or even reasonable maintenance. Unfortunately the restrictive zoning and rent control regulations for the low income residential parts of the city aggravate the cost of doing business in the rest of the city.

Without a doubt New York City faces formidable problems as it begins to face the twenty first century, but such problems notwithstanding, the economic base in the city is so strong that it may well survive for many years before the absence of any economic base can herald its retrenchment or even its demise. Chicago and San Francisco also have a great number of very strong industries which make up their economic base. Many other American cities are not so fortunate and as the factories which have made up the economic base for so many of these cities leave for more favorable rural locations, these urban centers must continuously be subsidized or eventually reach the same fate as other ghost towns in our country's history.

At the beginning of the twentieth century 14% of the American population lived in the city and only eleven cities in the world had populations of one million or more. Today, there are four hundred cities in the world with populations of a million or more and twenty urban centers with more than ten million. As cities around the world become more densely populated, cities in the United States are losing population. The typical city here is shaping up like a doughnut with emptiness in the center and growth in the suburbs and the rural periphery. Even though some cities are still thriving, of the 25 largest cities in 1950, 18 have lost population, e.g. Baltimore has lost 22% of its population between 1950 and 1994, Philadelphia 23%, Chicago 25%, Boston 28%, Detroit 44% and Cleveland 45%. Some cities have grown since 1950, but that is largely because they have annexed their outlying suburbs. As you might expect, New York City remains the same, but as we have already seen, this town has about the strongest economic base of any city in the U.S. In contrast to these trends, American suburbs have gained more than 75 million people in the same time period. We now have more people in the suburbs than in our cities.

Some scholars believe that the reason so many cities have fallen victim to urban blight is because the United States has made a series of public policy decisions that militate against the large cities. The one most often cited is the tax code which allows us to deduct mortgage interest and property taxes from the ordinary income that is taxable. The second is the fact that gasoline in the U.S. is cheaper than most other places in the world. The third is the allegation that public housing is concentrated in the major urban centers. The result of this is that the central cities have become the homes of the poor while the suburbs have become places to escape the poor. A fourth policy often cited is that the U.S. government neglects the big cities. The validity of these allegations is questionable at best and in many cases downright misleading.

First of all comparing American cities with cities in Europe and Japan is like trying to compare apples with oranges. In Europe and Japan people live in the urban centers and/or the metropolitan megalopolis because they have little or no choice. The countries as a whole are overpopulated and the governments with few exceptions control all of the vacant land and/or the development of any land. Income taxes are so severe in these countries and productivity so low that most consumer goods and especially new housing, is beyond the reach of the average citizen. The old bromide about gasoline taxes being high in Europe and Japan and practically non existent in the U.S. just doesn't wash with reality. Japan and the countries of Europe are so small that their economies can function very well with the limited amount of highway and street transportation that is available to them. Public transit serves these countries very well for the most part. By contrast transportation in the U.S. involves much greater mileage and traffic volumes. Distances between cities and market centers are vast compared to Europe and Japan. The distance from New York City to San Francisco is about the same as from the West coast of France to the Caspian Sea or the northern border of Iran or Saudi Arabia. The length of Japan is not as great as the distance from southern California to Oregon.

So many of our social scientist believe that the cause of our problems in our large urban centers is because of our divisions of race and income. Even though there may be some merit to this allegation, it is a poor substitute for the actual logistics which are the basis of peoples decisions to live and work where they want to live and are able to live and work. This does not mean that cities are "doomed". Old worn out and obsolete urban centers do not have to face the same fate as Carthage and be obliterated and the earth salted. They can change into new educational centers, parks and recreational centers or medical centers to mention only a few of the options. Rather than identifying such changes as a tragedy, it might be more beneficial to all concerned if planning could be started for the beginning of a new function of the old community location.

The formula for the survival and viability of our urban centers appears fairly clear based on their history. Notwithstanding the various sociological problems that seem concentrated in the large cities, the basic key to their solution as well as the overall viability of the city is a strong economic base, not government subsidies.

PART III

URBAN CENTERS FOR THE 21ᵀᴴ CENTURY

CHAPTER 10

AMERICA'S NEW URBAN CENTERS

Historically populations have always sooner or later responded to their needs and/or their compelling impulses for survival and improvement, and relocated to more advantageous circumstances and attractive environment. The current diaspora of American urbanites to the rural countryside is no exception to this historical pattern and for good reason. With the current state of political instability in the world supported by modern weapons that can reach any corner of the globe, combined with the hard times suffered by the central cities, which are also prime targets for the new weapons, the movement to the countryside has been accelerated by improvements in technology which makes the movement easier. An important question to resolve is what kind of town or community will result from these shifts in the demographics of America?

Rural America combined with modern technology offers the optimum setting for America's new communities. Starting with the country's most productive base, agriculture, and following with the movement of industry (manufacturing) to a rural environment, commercial and residential development are the natural result of America's dispersion or return to the farm. To thoroughly explain this movement it is important to understand what motivates Americans to improve their quality of life and also by what criteria we measure the quality of life. Without a doubt the impact of the environment on the human body affects the quality of life for that individual and we can identify that environment with the following criteria:

1. Freedom of movement (elbow room) and possession of a minimum amount of space about one's person is essential either in the home, the street, the workplace, the region or the community. It is a basic requirement for human comfort that we be able to create around ourselves an optimum protective

space. When we talk with each other, work together, sleep together, social-ize or function together in any manner, each time we seek an optimum dis-tance. This is also true of the rooms in our houses, buildings in our cities, work stations in the factory or office, seats in the airplane, bus or any other place where we must function with other people. For our comfort, we are concerned not with maximum or minimum distances, but the "optimum" distance.

2. Freedom from fear is fundamental to our well being. If there is any threat to our personal safety or the safety of our loved ones, the quality of life is diminished. This fear embraces everything from a vicious dog in the neigh-borhood to the potential for nuclear attack and of course criminal attacks on the streets of our cities.

3. Freedom from temperature extremes is most fundamental. Notwithstanding good clothing, good shoes and central heating and air conditioning, if its too hot or too cold, we are uncomfortable.

4. Clean air and good ventilation whether it be in the home, in the work place, in the store or in the street is essential. Bad odors, high concentrations of carbon dioxide, carbon monoxide and toxic or noxious fumes make us un-comfortable and over prolonged periods will make us sick and even shorten our lives.

5. Loud noises and dissonant sounds will destroy any sense of well being and may even undermine ones sanity. No matter what the source, off the street, in the work place or in the home, no human being can function with abnor-mal or untimely sounds for any extended length of time.

6. Pleasant and aesthetic appearances are essential for good mental health and a vigorous sense of well-being. Pervasive ugliness will eventually destroy any healthy frame of mind. Beauty is forever!

7. Satisfaction of performance and accomplishment although not a direct func-tion of the environment is indirectly impacted by the environment. As point-ed out by Arnold Toynbee, if the environment is too harsh, the best that can be accomplished by any culture is a state of arrested animation, e.g. the Eskimo culture in the arctic, the pygmy of central Africa or the Tuaregs of the Sahara. Correspondingly, the environment of the urban ghetto or the

continuous uncomfortablee life in a major urban center can undermine any feeling of satisfaction or hope of accomplishment.

8. Rest, relaxation and even recreation (as distinguished from entertainment) are well recognized elements of our well-being that must be supported by our environment. If the home or the community militate against this essential element, no person will long endure with such deprivation. Whether it be the walk through the zoo, the concert in the park, the occasional baseball or horseshoe game, or just plain quiet time in the backyard or the library, healthy diversion from the daily work schedule is necessary.

9. Freedom from excessive toil in providing the basic necessities of living, i.e. food, shelter, and clothing is essential for a healthy life and normal life span. Today's life style requires electric power, clean fuels, a well balanced food supply throughout the year and a four season wardrobe. In other words, we are no longer an agrarian culture so we cannot be expected to chop a winter's supply of cordwood for fuel, grow and can a years supply of fruit and vegetables or raise sheep and spin wool for our clothing.

10. Our environment must also provide us with the basic services for potable water, sanitary sewers, street maintenance, police and fire protection.

If these are some of the standards by which we measure our quality of life, how will the new communities in rural America satisfy these requirements? To accomplish these most important goals the communities must provide certain minimum facilities along with the basic municipal services. Typical services and facilities readily available to the community resident should be as follows:

1. Airport service.
2. Regional & neighborhood shopping centers with free parking.
3. Community college and/or education center with modern library.
4. Hospital, clinical, medical and dental services.
5. Primary and Secondary schools.
6. Day care centers for pre-school children.
7. Special education centers for handicappers.

9. Parks, zoos, swimming pools, tennis courts and/or nature centers.
10. Golf courses, bike paths, baseball and soccer fields.
11. Theaters, radio and cable television service.
12. Hotel-motels, restaurants and fast food service.
13. Interstate freeways and freeway access.
14. Balanced housing distribution including upper, middle and lower income single family detached, multifamily rental and condominium.
15. Repair services for automobiles, appliances and plumbers, electricians and carpenters.
16. Municipal services for fire protection, police protection, water and sewer services, trash and snow removal.

In the 19th century Mr. Louis Sullivan was the avant-garde architect for the design of the modern skyscraper. His famous credo "Form follows Function" became the guiding light for 20th century architecture. The converse of this axiom is perhaps closer to the truth. We are all too well aware of how Function follows Form. Although we may one way or another shape our buildings and communities, when we live our daily lives in them, we find that they shape us! Whether it be the house we live in, the automobile we drive, the desk or machine we work at, or the community we live in, the form and condition of these facilities dictates to a great extent how we behave and feel about ourselves, other people and the world.

Although the seeds of rural urbanization were firmly planted by 1950, the movement to the countryside began in earnest in the early seventies. Today it is taking place at an increasing rate in all but the most remote sections of the country. In most cases, but not all, the new communities have galvanized around rural villages and towns whose basic logistics and locations meet all or most of the criteria required for the growth of the 21st century "New Town". Here are some of the most outstanding criteria identifying the new communities:

1. The new community is located ten to fifty miles from an older and relatively large urban center. The larger urban center will be either a major

or a secondary town with a population of 100,000 to 500,000 people. It should be noted that many of these secondary urban centers are experiencing substantial rejuvenation if they have a well established economic base. Also note that commuting time to the workplace today is approximately 45 minutes.

2. At least one and in many cases two major interstate freeways serve the community for transportation to and from the major urban center. The new community is very automobile intensive. Rapid transit is provided by automobiles and interstate freeways.

3. Water supplies for domestic service and fire protection are provided by individual wells and/or extended municipal water distribution systems from the older villages.

4. Sanitary sewer service is provided by individual septic tanks and/or expanded sewage treatment facilities from the older community.

5. There is a centrally located medical clinic or outpatient hospital service. Specialized treatment services are available at the regional hospital usually located at a nearby primary or secondary urban center.

6. Elementary and secondary schools are available for the community and in many cases a Community College will be located in the vicinity. Here it should be noted that many colleges and universities are located in rural America and in fact have become a focal point for increased urbanization because of their own effort to encourage high tech industrial parks, research facilities for industry, etc.. Educational facilities including superior elementary and secondary schools are one of the most attractive elements in the urbanization of America.

7. Regional shopping malls with major anchor stores service the immediate area that are available within one hour commuting distance or up to fifty miles.

8. In many cases commercial and light industrial operations are located in or very near the new communities.

9. Municipal services, e.g. police and fire protection, street and road maintenance, social services and trash collection are provided by the county or the expanded services of the older small town. This may be the county sheriff,

local police department, volunteer or full time fire department, private contractor for trash collection, county social services, etc. The public library is often part of municipality and is an essential ingredient of a modern community.

10. Public utilities are provided by the easily expanded services of the regional electric power company and in most cases natural gas for fuel is provided by the regional gas company, both under the jurisdiction of the State Public Service Commission. In addition, telephone and television service with television cable services are available for almost unlimited service.

11. Properly zoned and well planned subdivisions of the land for residential, commercial, institutional and industrial use. Almost every state now has detailed laws and regulations for the subdivision of land so that the investment of the property owner is protected from poorly planned or unscrupulous development. The residential lot is protected from noise, intrusion of privacy, poor traffic access and good construction of streets and basic utilities. Commercial and industrial real estate investment is assured protection from infringement of zoning regulations and complaints from neighbors for the their operations.

12. Zoning, protective covenants and/or deed restrictions prevent any change in the use of the land. These instruments supported by law protect the owner's rights and his investment.

In fact, New Town, 21st Century, is here with us today and continues to grow and multiply. What is so important now is whether this growth and expansion will be healthy and prosperous or if it will become rigid and inflexible and thereby create its own obsolescence and deterioration for the future. This is what happened to so many of the older large urban centers created by the industrial revolution, but unable to change to adapt to the new technology. Today (and tomorrow) it is not the size of the city which makes the difference, but the level of cultural life within a geographical region that is important. A full cultural life depends on the freedom and stimulation of many kinds of encounters and personal choices rather than those choices dictated by a neglected or oppressive environment.

The new towns of 21st Century America will satisfy the needs and the preferences of the population and most importantly, be built on the technology of today and the future. By eschewing the burdens and unnecessary restrictions of obsolescent 19th century urban centers, New Towns will flourish and be nourished by new technology and the desire for more individual freedom from over regulation and more space to recreate. The focal point of necessary and/or desirable community activities will be the Community Centers and/or the schools. The regional shopping mall is also becoming an increasing center of community activities and may someday completely replace the municipal center.

With the new technologies industrial and commercial operations will continue to located in rural America with easy and convenient access to the New Towns. A most important characteristic of New Town will be its size. Unlike the densely populated urban centers of the 19th and 20th century, New Town will not need to be big and therefore will not be big. America still has a bountiful supply of open space and new technology now makes more of it available. Throughout nature all living things reach a certain size to satisfy the needs of the living organism. Any growth beyond this requirement becomes grotesque and ugly. So too will New Town reach its optimum size and to retain its charm and beauty, additional growth will be counterproductive and therefore will not be permitted. Where neglect and/or greed add such unnecessary growth to the town, it will appear as a cancer on the back of the community and if unchecked will destroy the town.

A very important feature of New Town which continue to grow and expand is the "Mall" and/or weather control. The concept of all retail stores being gathered together into a single complex of stores with pleasant surroundings, free parking and most importantly, climate control or protection from the extremes of the weather, is now well established all over the country. Added to this attractive community feature are all manner of restaurants from fast food to gourmet dinning along with entertainment centers with movie theaters, games and even child care for preschoolers. All of this makes for a most pleasant "Community Center" replacing the old up-town center on Main Street which was the most common characteristic of small towns in the 20th century.

The malls today are getting larger and are even connected together with other malls, parking structures with covered bridges and automatic movable side-walks.

If there were ever any doubts about the impact of technology on the way people live their lives, (function follows form) all one has to do is to visit any of today's (1996) modern regional shopping malls. With such a visit it becomes very clear that the urban center of today and for the 21st century is the Regional Mall. With easy access from the nation's interstate freeways, and of course all communities adjoining those freeways, convenient parking (free), total climate control inside the mall, complete shopping facilities with competitive pricing, food courts for any kind of dining, entertainment facilities including theatres, children's playgrounds, (there's even a swimming beach in West Edmonton, Alberta and a year around ice skating rink in the Galleria in Houston, Texas), and many other non retail shops and facilities. The Galleria in Houston has also added health clubs, banks, medical centers and brokerage houses. Other malls have added museums, libraries, branch offices of state and city offices. In one shopping mall in Ottawa the Board of Education has even added a store front classroom. In ancillary buildings outside of many malls it is not uncommon to see medical and dental offices and even large ticket items such as automobiles now have their showrooms very close to the malls.

The Mall of America may well be called the "avant guard" of shopping malls in America. Located in Bloomington, Minnesota, outside of Minneapolis the 4.2 million square foot mall is expected to draw more visitors than Walt Disney World or the Grand Canyon. During the first three months of its opening in 1992 nearly a million people a week visited the mall. The mall is very large. It has four department stores, about 360 specialty stores, more than forty restaurants and food outlets all of which are grouped around a seven acre glass roofed courtyard containing an amusement park with twenty two rides, two theatres, and many smaller attractions. There is a merry go round and even a roller coaster! Although the stores in the mall close at 10:00 P.M. the nightclubs on the fourth level stay open until 1:00 A.M. These clubs include a sports bar, comedy club. and country western supper club. The average visitor to a regional mall spends three hours there, but more than four hours in the Mall of America. Clearly this mall will be a trend setter for urban centers of the future.

The history of regional malls follows closely the history of technology. Parisian entrepreneurs originated the first department stores in the 1860s and they spread through Europe and America like wild fire. Shopping centers emerged in America in the early 1900s right after the turn of the century. Up to that time the suburbs were almost exclusively residential and all shopping was done "downtown" or "uptown" depending on what point of the compass the residential area was located from the urban center.

The Roland Park Shopping Center opened at the turn of the century five miles North of downtown Baltimore. This was followed by the First Market Square in Lake Forest near Chicago in 1916 and Country Club Plaza in Kansas City in 1925. The great depression and W.W. II slowed development of shopping centers and in 1946 there were only eight such centers in the United States.

The first modern regional mall appeared on the outskirts of Seattle, Washington in 1950. The mall was called Northgate and had an anchor store (department store) and a number of smaller stores and shops. It also had a gas station, drive-in bank and a movie theatre. Most importantly, it had a "free" 4,000 car parking lot! This was truly the beginning of convenient "one stop" shopping. In 1950 there were approximately 100 of these centers in the U.S.. By 1960 there were 3,700 of them and they were much bigger. In 1954 Northland, in the northern Detroit suburbs had a million square feet and free parking for 7,400 cars. Northland also included non retail offices, research laboratories, a hospital, residential apartments and a hotel. It was later called "edge city". America welcomed the shopping center with open arms. Not only the convenience and downright pleasant ambience of the new centers, but now one did not have to endure the dirty down towns with crowded streets, expensive parking and congested street traffic. It is also noteworthy that there are no panhandlers in the centers and the malls are much safer than the urban center streets.

In 1956 the first totally enclosed mall was built in Edina, Minnesota with air conditioning in the common areas in the summer and heated during the winter.

The most dramatic innovation here was that all of the public areas in the mall were totally enclosed and air conditioned. One could move from store to store, store to restaurant, restaurant to theatre and theatre to coffee shop with complete comfort. No overcoat, umbrella or boots would ever be required until you went to the parking lot and in some of the malls, even the parking lot was covered. The parking structure was coming into its own in a big way and most importantly, the parking was free! From 1960 to 1970 more than 8,000 new shopping centers opened in the United States, double the number from the previous decade. Most of these followed the example of Southdale Center in Edina and provided total enclosure of the public areas. In the 1980s the malls got even larger and now multi-story became the norm which shortened the walking between stores. One, two and three million square feet have become common for the regional mall and the biggest of them all, West Edmonton Mall in Alberta provides 5.2 million square feet of covered space. From 1970 to 1990 almost 25,000 new shopping centers were built in the United States. When these malls added such things as athletic clubs, banks, medical centers and offices to the main retail functions, people began to think of the malls as primary urban centers. A high school even added classrooms to the mall in Ottawa.

Most significantly, what enables these malls to be built and to function for the comfort, convenience and entertainment of the customer, is modern technology. Air conditioning, modern lighting, elevators and escalators with moving sidewalks, and of course the automobile, all permit the modern design, construction and operation of these super mall-urban centers. Remember, as little as sixty years ago such facilities were practically impossible to construct and operate. Up until that time as a practical matter, all rooms had to have windows which could admit light and ventilation air. Some of the large department stores and some offices had introduced electric lighting and forced air ventilation for large interior spaces, but the vast bulk of architectural buildings still relied on windows and skylights for light and air for the stores, offices, factories, apartments and single family housing. Air conditioning, modern lighting and elevators have changed all of this design. Today an entire shopping center, factory or office building can be designed and built without any exterior windows! The controlled environment is now the standard.

The regional shopping centers have become so popular with the American public that they now appear as the modern "downtown" or urban center in the minds of many people. This is especially true where the malls include many non commercial tenants, i.e. tenants other than retail stores. The question has even been raised that such malls are no longer "private" property, but public space subject to all the rules and regulations of public property! The issue is far from settled. Such issues as public access, free speech, political demonstrations, etc., fly in the face of private property rights and will have many court hearings before the rules are established. Even the U.S. Supreme Court and several State Supreme Courts have ruled on these questions, but they are still far from settled. One thing is certain, the enclosed regional mall is rapidly becoming the urban center in America.

CHAPTER 11

HOUSING FOR RURAL URBANIZATION IN THE 21ST CENTURY

Housing design and construction for the communities of New Town has never been more important than it is today. Today's housing for all of America, as well as New Town, must fit the culture of the 21st century. Not only must the house meet the basic code requirements and family needs, it must also satisfy the technological requirements and life style of Americans in this new culture. The American culture of the 21st century will be very different than the culture of the 20th century. At the beginning of the 20th century the U.S. population was 76.212 million; in 1930 it was 123.202 million and in 1990 it was 248.710 million. In the year 2,040 assuming a 2% growth per year, the population will be on the order of 670 million people. Obviously, a tremendous amount of American life style will change to accommodate this increase of population. Housing will be one of the most significant changes. When 50% to 80% of the individual's time is spent in the home and the small area around the home, the importance of this space cannot be over emphasized.

Good housing design must begin with good zoning regulations for the use of the land where the house is to be built. Along with protecting the property and its investment from bad environment and construction and improper or poor use of the property, good zoning establishes the population density and the corresponding design parameters of the house itself. No one wants the government dictating how someone must live their private lives, but in the interest of the Public Health and Welfare, the protection of the homeowners investment and the well being of each individual, Public Policy must set forth minimum standards for the habitat and its environment. Without such standards architectural anarchy, disease and economic chaos will result. This is especially important considering the great increases in population we can anticipate in the next fifty years. Unfortunately, this problem is all too evident in so many of our inner cities today.

Multiple families living in a single family dwelling will soon devastate a housing project. It should be pointed out here that political freedom notwithstanding, a major factor in the creation of slum housing in our major urban centers has been the flagrant disregard of density control regulations as well as the enforcement of Building Codes. Up to this time Housing Codes, which are different than Building Codes, have seldom if ever been enforced and in most cases not even adopted in most parts of the country.

The types of buildings used for housing range from single family detached dwellings to multi-family high rise apartment buildings. Frequently a housing development will consist of only one type of housing, but in a large development a mix of several types will occur. Zoning regulations usually allocate one type of housing to one area which will be contiguous to another type of housing area with another type contiguous to it, etc.. Planning considerations such as dwelling densities, type of occupancy, value of the land, size of houses, etc. will dictate the actual type of housing for a given area in the community. It should be noted that nothing in a Housing Code or a Building Code speaks to the community planning about private nonresidential properties such as stores, factories, schools, etc. and how they are mixed in with residential homes. Nor does the Housing Code speak to the public lands such as parks, libraries, fire and police stations, playgrounds, zoos etc.. Housing types can be divided into several basic categories:

1. *Single-Family Detached.* These houses are located on separate lots and are designed to accommodate a single family. A single American family generally means a group of two to eight people made up of adults and children. The mix may vary considerably. The houses are owner occupied for the most part, but rental units are not uncommon.

2. *Single-Family Attached.* This type of house is made up of two or more dwelling units attached to each other with a common wall. Each dwelling unit is designed to accommodate a single American family. This group includes duplexes, quadruplexes, row houses and town houses. This type of

housing is usually located on a single large lot and may be owner occupied or rental units.

3. *Garden Apartments.* These dwelling units are usually two to three story apartment buildings with higher densities (i.e. more dwelling units per acre.) and are most often, but not always, rental units.

4. *High-Rise Apartments.* The buildings for these dwelling units are usually seven stories and higher and have the greatest density of dwelling units per acre. Because high rise buildings are more expensive to build, these buildings are almost always located on high priced land.

5. *Mobile Homes.* Although these are single family detached dwelling units built in a factory, they are not constructed to the same standards as conventional "stick-built" housing. Many mobile homes are located in parks and on scattered lots throughout rural America. Most of these parks are located in high density mobile home parks and unfortunately too many of them are permitted to be built on flood plains with very poor flood histories. Once these homes are moved from the factory and located on a lot with a hook-up to all of the utilities, they are seldom if ever moved again. A mobile home is usually purchased with a chattel mortgage since it is considered personal property by mortgage companies and other lending institutions. Legally it is also considered personal property. However, the lot and foundations where the mobile home is set is real property and this is usually rented by the home owner.

In recent years the Condominium type of ownership has become popular in lieu of the more traditional fee-holder title to the property. Any of the housing units outlined above may be owned as a condominium and this type of ownership offers many attractive advantages to the owner.

In addition to the zoning ordinances, the Building Codes provide the highest degree of protection for the home owner and/or the home renter. The purpose of the Building Code is to protect life and limb, but not property! What should also be emphasized is that the Code establishes "minimum" standards for design, materials and workmanship. The Building Code does not speak to higher quality of construction or materials. If standards higher than what the Code requires are desired, then the higher standards must be set forth in individual contracts and specifications for the agreements between the buyer and the builder. It should also be pointed out that in some areas of the country there are no Building Codes of jurisdiction. Any housing or other building construction in these areas should be purchased with the Code embraced in the purchase agreement for the minimum standards to which the structure must be built. With so much development now occurring in rural America, the State should be very busy mandating these minimum standards for "all" rural areas in any given region of the country.

With safety in mind the Building Codes set standards for access and egress requirements, space limits for fire breaks, materials and methods of construction, plumbing, heating and air conditioning and electrical standards for illumination, power and safety. Most importantly, the Building Code is "not" the Housing Code. The Housing Code usually embraces a Building Code for its construction standards, but its primary goal is to set minimum standards for the utilization of space for housing. Space standards for occupancy for bedrooms, food preparation areas, closet space, corridors, ceiling heights, window and ventilation requirements, heating and electrical power standards, etc. are established in the Code for single-family detached housing or multi-family housing. Many regions of the country do not have a housing code and for that matter many regions of the country do not have a Building Code. For further reference to these subjects the individual codes should be consulted. There are four basic model housing codes that have been developed in the United States. They are:

1. "Recommended Housing Maintenance and Occupancy Ordinance" by the American Public Health Association (APHA).
2. "The Basic Housing Code" by the Building Officials Conference of America (BOCA).
3. "The Southern Standard Housing Code" by the Southern Standard Building Code Conference (S.S.B.C.C.).
4. "Housing Code" by the International Conference of Building Officials (I.C.B.O.).

There is general uniformity with most of the codes with regard to occupancy requirements and the habitable floor area per person as shown on the following table.

Dwelling Unit Occupancy Requirements

(Floor Area In Square Feet)

Code	1 Person	2 Persons	3 Persons	4 Persons	5 Persons
APHA	150	250	350	450	550
BOCA	150	250	350	450	550
ICBO	200	200	290	330	380
Southern	150	250	350	450	525

However there are substantial differences in the current standards for the total floor area requirements. The total floor area requirements include the additional space needed for halls, laundry, foyers, bathrooms, furnace rooms, closets, etc.. The APHA in 1950 recommended the following minimum standards:

Minimum Total Floor Area

1-Person	400 s.f.
2-Persons	750 s.f.
3-Persons	1,000 s.f.
4-Persons	1.150 s.f.
5-Persons	1,400 s.f.
6-Persons	1,550 s.f.

Many Housing Codes if they exist at all, have failed to keep up with modern standards of ventilation or electrical power and lighting improvements. Every resident of any community in the United States is entitled to know that the house he or she has purchased has been constructed according to nationally recognized standards. The Building Code is the standard of construction for any building. The Housing Code is the standard for residential occupancy which also embraces the standards of the Building Code for construction by reference. Housing Codes usually apply to all structures that are used for human habitation and dwellings. This would include not only single-family detached or attached houses, apartments, but also hotels, dormitories, jails, camps, etc.. Mobile homes, ships at sea, rail road pullman cars, travel trailers and campers are not covered by the Housing Codes. In general it might be said that the Housing Code describes what is to be provided for residential housing as compared with the Building Code which describes how the structures are to be constructed. A typical Housing Code addresses the following subjects:

EXTERIOR PROPERTY AREAS. This will embrace Sanitation, Noxious Weeds, Fences, Out Buildings including garages, Vacant Property, Sidewalks, Driveways, Patios and other similar improvements contiguous to the house.

INTERIOR & EXTERIOR STRUCTURAL MAINTENANCE. This will include Foundations, Walls and Roofs, Doors, Windows, Porches, Stairs, Fire Escapes, Kitchen and Bathroom floors and halls, Structural Maintenance in general.

SANITATION, INSECTS, RODENTS, ANIMAL, VERMIN & DAMPNESS. This part of the code speaks directly to Sanitation, Freedom from Dampness, Insect and Rodent Harborage, Guards for basement windows, Dogs, cats, birds, wild animals and even horses.

REQUIRED EQUIPMENT & FACILITIES. Minimum Kitchen Facilities, Privacy for Flush Toilets, Bathtubs & Showers, Space Heating Facilities, Potable Water Supplies, Hot Water Supplies, Plumbing for Sewer Systems, Electrical Wiring and Lighting Fixtures, Storage Space, Hardware for Locksets.

LIGHT & VENTILATION   Natural Light and Ventilation in Habitable Rooms including Kitchens and Bathrooms and Non Habitable Space.

SPACE & ROOM ARRANGEMENTS. Here are standards for minimum space for Habitable Rooms, Traffic Flow from Room to Room, Ceiling Heights, Maximum Number of people per Dwelling Unit, Location of Bath & Sleeping Rooms and Prohibited Occupancies.

FIRE PROTECTION. This section will include Means of Egress, Required Window Exits for Sleeping Rooms, Stairs and Other Verticle Openings, Fire Escapes, Fuel Burning Equipment, Smoke and Fire Alarm Systems and Interior Finishes.

This outline describes some, but not all, of the standards embraced in a typical Housing Code. It is probably safe to say that most communities in the U.S. either do not have such a code or they do not enforce it if it is on the books. Any new community would be very wise to adopt such a code if they wish to avoid many of the problems of the older urban centers in America.

Probably the most important standard of any Housing Code is the amount of space allocated to the housing unit for a single family dwelling. The current standards which evolved during the 20th century include not only the space needed for habitable rooms, but also the space needed for closets, hallways, utilities, laundry, etc.. These standards would include the following elements:

1. Living and/or family room.
2. Dinning room or eating space.
3. Kitchen, food storage & preparation.
4. Bedrooms or sleeping space.
5. Hallways, stairs and legal exits.
6. Bathrooms & Powder Rooms.
7. Closet & storage space.
8. Laundry rooms.
9. Utility room for space heating, electrical switchgear and hot water heating.

10. Garage and other out buildings for automobiles & maintenance
    equipment.

Although there is some variation in the amount of space allocated for each
individual function because of dual use of some of the space, the summary of
space for current single-family dwelling units might be:

Gross Space Standards for 20th Century Dwelling Units

Unit efficiency	Low	Medium	Luxury	HUD	GARAGE/ PARKING SPACE
(1-bath)	450 s.f.	500-550 s.f.	600+s.f.	380 s.f.	1-parking space
1-Bedroom (1-bath)	650 s.f.	700-800 s.f.	900+s.f.	580 s.f.	1-parking space
2-Bedroom (2-bath)	950 s.f.	1100-1200 s.f.	1250+s.f.	750 s.f.	2-car garage
3-bedroom (2-bath)	1250 s.f.	1350-1450 s.f.	1600+s.f.	900 s.f.	2-car garage + storage

However, housing for the beginning of the 21st century will need more
space to accommodate the life style and requirements of living in rural America.
The most important additions to the space standards outlined above are space
for office and library requirements, and space for additional automobile and/or
commuting vehicle storage along with a disaster room. Office space is needed

not only for the increasing administrative burden required for the operation of a household, but especially for the increasing number of breadwinners who work out of their home. This standard applies to lower income housing as well as upper income housing.

An important addition to the 21st century home should be a "disaster shelter", which in most cases would be a basement room or any other underground storm cellar. The room should have adequate structural integrity with radiation protection, emergency exits and emergency lighting, food and water supplies, plumbing facilities, first aid kits, blankets and telecommunication equipment including short wave sets. The structural make up of the walls, floors and ceilings should provide protection from radiation of nuclear attacks as well as biological attacks and supplies should be provided to last at least one week if not one month of habitation. This room should be designed, built and furnished to cope with the following emergencies:

1. Severe Weather
2. Nuclear Bomb Attacks
3. Biological Warfare Attacks

Attacks with nuclear and biological weapons may come from any foreign power or from any malcontent terrorist. We must remember that these weapons are very portable and much less expensive than conventional military armaments. Design requirements for such a "disaster room" should include:

1. Adequate space for the family
2. Potable water supply.
3. Second access and exit.
4. Toilet and shower.
5. Food supply.
6. Telecommunications and supply of batteries.
7. First Aid kits and supply of prescription medicine.
8. Blankets, towels and clothes for the family.
9. Auxiliary lighting and power supply (generator).
10. Auxiliary fuel supply.

Remember, in an emergency, electric power is most often shut down, streets may not be passable because of fallen trees and grocery stores and gas stations are cleaned out.

When Americans live in the new communities of rural America in the 21st century their new homes must not only measure up to the standards of the 21st century, but their economic viability must be maintained to support the new home and the new community. Bearing in mind that today the new home in the new community in the countryside is located so that the commute to work is less than one hour (45 min is normal today.) since so much of industry is already located in the rural locations all over America. Along with this trend is the increasing number of breadwinners working out of their own home! Because of new computer technology, namely the microchip, executive and administrative operations can easily be directed from home for many industries. With lap-top computers agricultural, transportation, manufacturing and professional directions can even be made from an airplane, automobile or the home. Electronic mail (E-mail) has already made a serious impact on the revenue of the U.S. Post Office. One consequence of this fairly recent communication capability has been the development of the rural Office Park as well as the expansion of the number of offices in the home.

In addition to the home office being used to earn a living, an office in the home is almost a requirement for the management of the house. Whether it be financial planning (including taxes), family health and medical records, scheduling for school affairs, planning for meals, maintenance of automobiles and home equipment, vacation, holidays or civic affairs, a home office work station is almost a necessity. The work station must provide space for a desk, telephone and in some cases a FAX machine, personal computer and typewriter, file cabinets ,library shelves and plenty of storage space to say the least. All together a special room is now needed in the house for these important operations. This is especially true if the breadwinner also earns his or her living with an office in the home.

For the "home" office function a minimum of 50 square feet with an average of 125 s.f., should be added to the standards for housing in the 21st century. Electric power and illumination should also be increased to accommodate the new equipment and special furniture should also be made available for the residential office. Commercial office furniture just doesn't fit into a private home properly. Following are some, but not necessarily all, of the operations and equipment for the home office.

1. Preparation of correspondence and memoranda.
2. Telephone, answering machine and FAX machine.
3. Personal computer and program storage.
4. Reference book, magazine and periodical storage.
5. File cabinets for legal and standard size documents, correspondence and records. A fire proof file should also be provided for security of important records.
6. Bulletin board and calendar.
7. A working desk (as opposed to a decorative piece of furniture.)
8. A desk chair for computer operation (as opposed to an executive or judges chair.)
9. A reading chair and lamp.
10. Closet storage for paper, office supplies and equipment.

These are minimum essentials for a home office. To function best the space should be provided as a separate room with a door for privacy, security and acoustical integrity. It is very important that good mechanical ventilation be provided for this space.

In addition, if the breadwinners of the family will work out of the home either part or full time, additional space will be required "as needed" for such operations as:

1. Additional library shelves.
2. Additional file cabinets.
3. Work tables or drafting tables.
4. Plan file cabinets.
5. Photocopy machines.
6. Special equipment, e.g. easels, postage machines, etc.
7. Reception area and visitor furniture.

8.   Additional parking for visitors and deliveries.

This list could easily be expanded depending on the nature of the "home business" and the zoning limitations for businesses operated from the home. In any event it is clear that conventional housing design (20th century) must increase the amount of space provided for the home to meet the standards of the 21st century. Total housing minimum floor area standards should therefore be increased by at least 25% and hopefully even more to accommodate the additional requirements of the next century. Standards for construction will also change. Building Code officials are constantly revising the codes to keep up with modern technology and the development of new problems. New technology just in recent years has brought us many new materials which have not yet gained wide acceptance, but will undoubtedly see wider and better use with their application to building technology. Pre-stressed concrete and plastic pipe are just a few of the new products which have entered the marketplace in the last fifty years and are finally gaining more popular acceptance.

Most importantly for the new towns and the urbanization of rural America the great increases in the general population in the next century will force many substantive changes in the materials we use and the way we build our houses. With just the addition of 420 million people to the general population in the next fifty years, something like 75 to 85 million dwelling units will have to be added to house this great number of people. Everyone has to live somewhere. Existing methods of building housing will have a great deal of difficulty meeting such demand. Manufactured housing which meets the requirements of Building and Housing Codes, is called Modular Housing to distinguish the industry from the mobile home industry. And even though the Modular Housing industry could meet the production demands for such a great number of houses, many state and federal banking laws will have to change to allow the economics of the industry to operate with favorable returns on investment. Along with such changes in the laws of finance, new materials will have to be used to avoid depletion of our forest reserves. Steel and aluminum framing members to replace lumber as well as plastic to replace copper for the plumbing to mention just a few of the many material changes.

One outstanding advantage for America is the vast amount of land available for development. Up to this time the biggest limitation for the use of this land surplus has been the limited supply of water and sewer services. Here again new technology should provide the new remedies for this problem and allow the development and expansion of the economy to move ahead

CHAPTER 12

21ST CENTURY URBANIZATION IN THE UNITED STATES & THE WORLD

With the advent of new discoveries and the improvement of old technologies of the 20th century we may expect radical changes in the development of new urban centers not only in the United States, but in Canada, North Africa, Australia, the Gobi Desert and Brazil, South America. Note, Canada is probably the most underdeveloped country in the world. The common denominator for all of these locations (except the U.S.) is that today they represent most of the underdeveloped land in the world. The reason these areas are underdeveloped at this time is either the lack of water, the extreme climate or both. With the population of the world expected to double in the next twenty five years and then double again in the following twenty five years, new habitat and new food supplies will be essential to accommodate this enormous increase in world populations. With as little growth as 3% per year, the United States will have a population of nearly 700 million by the middle of the 21st century! Since these populations were the result of modern technology, it is only fitting that technology provide the means to sustain these increases. And so it will as long as people let the technology work for them and not against them.

The earth is blessed with a super abundance of water. Its only shortcoming is that most of this water contains too much salt and/or enormous quantities of sweet water is locked up in the polar ice caps and the atmosphere over the oceans. The engineering challenge of course is to convert this tremendous water resource to potable and useable water supplies and transport the water to the agricultural and populations centers of the world. We know how to remove the salt from the sea water and we know how to melt the snow on the glaciers and ice caps. We even think we know how to move some of the water from the atmosphere. But we do not yet know how to do any of this efficiently or economically. Once water is reclaimed from these resources it must be transported to where it is economically useful. Water from the Pacific Ocean and the Gulf of Mexico must be transported to the deserts and semi-arid prairies of Canada, the U.S. and Mexico. Such transportation can be more costly than desalinization.

The main solution to these heavy engineering problems is low cost energy. As we enter the 21st century we have a remedy for this problem with nuclear power. Today the main problem with this bountiful supply of energy is political and/or economic self interest, but the political and powerful economic self interest of fossil fuels will have to yield to the overwhelming demands for more water and more inexpensive fuel for the next century. We also know that there are enormous reserves of heat energy deep in the earth near the earth's core and when we learn how to tap this great reservoir we will have a second source of thermal energy. Fossil fuels, coal, oil and gas will be obsolete in the 21st century.

There is also more than enough evidence to show that the shortage of water will foment more wars and political strife than we have seen for the last several hundred years. In the 13th century Genghis Kahn conquered most of Asia, eastern Europe and the Middle East when the fertile grasslands of the Asian steppes had turned into the present day Gobi desert after the dramatic climate change of the 8th and 9th century. No doubt the poor food supply enabled Genghis to mobilize the mongols and many other tribes and/or nations to seek greener pastures in the West. The range wars of the western United States were practically all over water and today one of the most sensitive and explosive political situations in the Middle East can find the roots of most of their problems in the meager supply of fresh water available to the desert lands of Palestine and the Levant. Production of food is directly proportional to the water supply available. When water is not available or restricted, food is not available or restricted. In the 21st century water will be much more precious than oil. Correspondingly, as these economic pressures demand more low cost energy and nuclear power is used more and more, fossil fuels namely coal and oil will no longer be in demand and severe economic dislocations will result. On the brighter side we may look forward to cleaner air to breathe and seeing the world reforested with the demand for fuel now satisfied by nuclear or geothermal energy in lieu of coal, gas, oil, wood and charcoal.

Its important to remember that up until the 19th century wood was our exclusive supply of fuel for cooking food and space heating. By the beginning of the 20th century the forest of Europe, the Middle East, Asia and many parts of Africa were denuded and almost extinct. The discovery of coal and then oil provided some relief which saved much of the forest land from turning into sandy deserts, but the forest are still being wasted and eliminated in much of the overdeveloped parts of the world. Only a cheaper and more economical source of energy will save these forest from complete annihilation. Even today our satellites can measure how rapidly the forest of Africa and South America are being depleted and replaced by deserts and of course starvation has already overtaken millions of people who depended on this land for their fuel and food supply.

It is very difficult and even foolish to argue with simple arithmetic. More people will require more food and to produce more food more water will be required where the food is to be grown and temperatures will have to be moderated to extend the growing season where required. This requires economical supplies of fuel and energy which will be supplied by better technology. As new lands are developed with more water and temperature controls, new urban centers will be developed to accommodate the new agricultural industries in these new locations. These new population shifts will cause political disruptions. Notwithstanding any political changes, economic obsolescence or population shifts, people will still have to eat and food will be produced where it is most economical to grow food and this means where water will be available and the climate may be modified to enhance the growing seasons.

Along with many improvements to our existing technology there will be many major new additions to the technology of the 21st century that will have a maximum impact on our urban centers and the way we live our lives. Some of the technological changes we may expect to see in the next century are:

1. A new sea level canal to replace the Panama Canal. We may also expect to see substantial improvements in submarines for the movement of goods from China and Japan underneath the polar ice caps to Europe.

2, Accelerated melt of the northern polar cap to provide irrigation water for the plains of North America and Asia. This will be accomplished primarily by the use of nuclear energy, geothermal mines and solar melt techniques (lampblack).

3. Irrigation of the central plains of the United States with desalinated water from the Pacific and the Gulf of Mexico to replace the depleted Ogala aquifer at the center of the North American continent.

4. Electric powered automobiles and trucks to replace the internal combustion engine. The familiar gas station will disappear from the urban and rural scene.

5. "Bullet" trains between major urban centers with speeds of 300 to 400 mph. Transportation between major urban centers will be almost exclusively by these high speed trains with air travel restricted to routes of 1,000 miles or more. Local transportation will be provided by electrically powered commuter cars and buses from the transportation centers to suburbs and residences. All local transportation will be controlled electronically including speed, route selection, etc. Modern 20th century airports will of course be obsolete and the new "train" stations of the 21st century will be a hallmark of the new American urban center.

6. A "seaway" canal through the ice of the Great Lakes to permit year around shipping from Duluth to the Atlantic Ocean. (the present St. Laurence seaway can only be used six or seven months of the year because of the winter ice.)

7. "Safe" nuclear power plants to replace all fossil fuel power plants located at least 100 miles from the urban centers (load centers).

8. Practical shoes and clothing to provide comfort and freedom from disease for everyone.

9. Genetic engineering for the elimination of genetically acquired diseases including but not limited to heart disease, diabetes, stroke, arthritis and high blood pressure. We will also see a new industry develop for the

manufacture of body replacement parts including but not limited to hearts, kidneys, lungs, livers and maybe even some parts of the brain including eyes for the restoration of sight and hearing for the deaf! By the end of the next century we should see the life span of the human being extended to 150 years!

10. Alteration of ocean currents and warm water movements (El Nino) with hurricane and tornado modification. These changes will also add to and increase rainfall in the Sahara and Gobi deserts. To optimize these changes major passage ways through the Himalayas and the Rocky Mountain chains may be installed to allow improved atmospheric weather movements in the northern hemisphere.

11. Colonization of the Moon and probably Mars with development of industrial, mining and astronomical exploration bases. This will include operational stations on the moon for the control of weather, environmental quality and telecommunications on the earth. Recent investigations of the lunar surface suggest that water (frozen) may be present on the moon.

12. Genetic engineering to increase food production for grains, fruits, fodder and in particular, ocean based vegetation for human consumption. Food supplies and preparation will change. Food preservation technology will allow residential and commercial storage for much longer periods, e.g. 6 months to five years. The beef industry as we know it today (1996) will be replaced by the buffalo industry. Agriculture will no longer have to be subsidized to support the grain and beef business. Food grown and harvested from the sea (not fish) will provide most of the food for the world. Many deserts will be converted to productive agricultural land with irrigation from desalinization plants. The economics of this new water supply and transportation of the water will not permit the marginal land which has been subsidized in the U.S. for many years to continue growing substandard grain and cattle forage in the U.S.

13. A substantial increase in the number of manufacturing factories built totally underground with roof tops serving as parking lots, golf courses and parks. Note since most new factories today are completely air conditioned the next step of placing them completely underground is most logical so as to make

the most optimum use of the land. It should also be noted that all buildings built on the Moon or on Mars will have to be built underground because of the extreme climatic conditions.

14. Money, i.e. currency, may disappear entirely as a medium of exchange. In its place we will probably find electronic transfer, the credit card and PIN number used for all but the smallest transactions of trade and commerce.

15. Since all prime power will be electric, especially for automobiles and home heating, the all too familiar gas station will disappear from the American highway scene and overhead electric power and telephone lines will also become a relic of the past.

16. With electric automobiles and the further development of the micro chip we will probably see the elimination of traffic lights since street and highway traffic will be controlled electronically as will the apprehension of speeding and/or unauthorized vehicles by the police. In this regard we may also see the automobile computer programmed for its destination from its home to the grocery store, the office, grandmother's house or the vacation beach, thus eliminating the need for the driver at the wheel. Commercial and industrial trucking will travel mostly at night (low traffic volume) and in most cases drivers will not even be required for the long hauls between urban and industrial centers. Note, except for the smallest details most large aircraft, military aircraft and guided missiles are operated with automatic pilots and inertial guidance systems today.

17. Interstate highways and other freeways will of course have to be redesigned to accommodate this method of travel and reservations may well have to be made to avoid overloading the highway circuits for high volume traffic. Buses, commercial and industrial trucking will of course have their own highway lanes to accommodate their heavy loads and will not share the passenger lanes with automobiles. With low cost energy for electric snow and ice removal mechanical snow removal from the freeways will be obsolete.

18, Automobile design and construction will change to not only accommodate the new electric fuel supply, but also to be compatible with the new traffic control systems, and the change of styles for local and long range

transportation, e.g. more lounge space, office space, sleeping and minimized driver requirements.
19. One of the most significant changes in housing will be the addition of the domestic waste treatment units and the corresponding elimination of sanitary sewers and/or the requirements for soil that can "perk" for the classical rural septic tank. With this change, development of housing will no longer be limited to sanitary sewer availability, so houses may literally be built anywhere a water supply is available.
20. New materials and structural engineering designs will be developed to enclose hundreds or even thousands of acres of land without the interruptions of intermediate columns so that entire cities and urban centers will be covered and protected from the elements.

These are some, but certainly not all of the technological improvements we might look forward to in the next century.

With such an array of new technological advances in the next century what kind of urban centers will we have to house, feed, entertain, employ and educate our future populations?

First of all it is important to realize that our "new" urban centers will not be located where the urban centers of the 20th century are located. As new technology shifts the location of such things as food production, manufacturing of goods and services, transportation routes and centers, etc., the new urban centers will also develop at these new locations. Older urban centers may well continue to serve well as long as they adapt to and are compatible with the new technology and most importantly, they retain their economic base which will support their population. Their are thousands of ghost towns in America left over from the 19th and early 20th century which lost their economic base and then disappeared into history. Of necessity government subsidizing of cities will become a thing of the past except for a few historic locations, e.g. Washington D.C., Philadelphia, New York, San Francisco, etc. and only the artistic and historic parts of these great cities will be preserved with subsidized funds. These locations may even be designated national parks.

The focal point of the new urban centers will be their transportation centers which of course will be connected to the transportation arteries connecting the urban center to other urban centers, industrial centers, utility centers, airports, etc. The urban center itself will be totally enclosed not unlike today's modern shopping malls. The center will include major centers for shopping, hospital services, colleges and universities, entertainment theatres, e.g. movies, baseball and football fields, opera houses; residential apartments, office buildings, libraries, museums, police and fire departments and municipal offices. Local transportation within the center will be via moving sidewalks and/or electric buses and cars not unlike today's electric golf carts. Suburban developments in the vicinity of the major urban center may or may not be totally enclosed depending on the climate of the region. If enclosed, the suburban pods will have a transportation artery connecting the suburb to the major urban center not unlike our freeways of today. Within the enclosed suburban pod will be single family homes of course, parks, golf courses, small shopping centers, churches, temples and mosques, primary and secondary schools, libraries, police and fire departments and municipal offices. Since the climate will be totally controlled, grass, trees and other vegetation will flourish the year around and wild life should enjoy the same comforts. Severe weather, blizzards, tornadoes, hurricanes, etc. should not be a problem for any of the urban centers.

A different concept of work should prevail in the next century. Except for basic services, e.g. electrician, telecommunication repairs, carpenters, plumbers, etc., manufacturing, mining, agriculture and a great deal of construction will be by robots with controls by computers. As far as the urban centers are concerned including the suburban centers, most of this production will be controlled from the offices in the homes of the urban and rural residents as well.

Most importantly, the power plants, factories, mines and farms will not be located "in" the urban centers. Underground factories will be located in their separate enclosed pods with their transportation arteries connecting them to the urban centers and their supplier factories and warehouses. It should be noted that some of the factories today can be completely operated by robots and human beings are not needed on the factory floor. In fact artificial lighting is not even needed for these factories. Robots don't need to see! An industrial pod might include either one or several "industrial parks". One benefit of such developments is that air and water pollution will be entirely eliminated. All air and water used in the manufacturing process will be completely treated and then recycled after its use in the manufacturing process. The roofs of large manufacturing plants that are built underground will be used for parking and or parks and golf courses or if the property becomes too expensive this "roof" land may be used for offices and/or transportation centers.

The layout of a regional urban center will therefore appear similar to the geometry of a snowflake with the major center in the middle and the transportation arteries connecting the smaller centers to the major. We may visualize the North American continent covered with a pattern of such snow flake design all connected to each other with transportation arteries for the rail roads and all vehicular traffic. The interstitial spaces between the centers should all be colored green with the greatly improved growth of trees and other vegetation. The whole not unlike what the land must have been in the 15th century.

Since our culture is based on technology and in fact driven by technology, we can anticipate substantial changes in our social fabric as a result of the technological advances in the 21st century. Most conspicuous perhaps will be the absence or at least substantial changes of some common features of the 20th century landscape. Some of the social changes we might see in the 21st century would be:

1. As much as one third or even one half of the work force will work out of the home. Housing will have to be designed to accommodate this new use which will include office space, three and four car garages, entertainment centers, closed circuit TV and educational facilities.

2. As much as one half of elementary, secondary and university education will be in the home. One of the most substantive changes will be that the standard school year will be 12 months instead of the 20th century traditional 9 months. One of the most significant changes will be that the public school will no longer be the laboratory of social engineering for the shaping of physical, psychological and political experiments. Teaching will

be by closed circuit television with the most outstanding scholars with the best credentials and the classrooms will be expanded to thousands instead of the traditional 25 or 30 students. With the exception of a few select laboratory classes, all teaching will be by television and the monitors will not have to have teaching credentials. This will not only reduce the cost of education (reducing the number of expensive teachers), but will radically change the design and construction of the typical school and classroom. Teachers will have to increase their credentials for basic technical skills, e.g. math, geography, English, history, etc., and school administrators will have to deal with a different set of problems with much more television programming, reduced food services, elimination of mass busing for students (or at least a 50% reduction of in house students) and practically no interscholastic sports. Title IX and high insurance cost will eliminate football and possibly baseball from high school athletics. Extra curricular activities, athletics, clubs, plays, etc., will use public facilities, e.g. libraries, community centers, parks, etc.. Property taxes will change accordingly. The school will therefore be more of a TV studio with top quality teaching programs being purchased or rented for the classroom session. Note, one such program may serve many school districts, again and again and again substantially reducing the high labor cost of professional teachers.

3.   The three car garage and even the four car garage will be common for single family detached housing.

4.   The automobile dealership with its 20th century style of showroom, used car lot, service shop, body shop, parts department and car storage lot will essentially disappear like the 19th century blacksmith shop. Electric powered cars will be marketed more like household appliances from major shopping malls. With far fewer moving parts much less service and maintenance will be required and repairs will be primarily by house calls from electrical repair men for service and parts replacement. Because of new materials, mostly plastics, and commonality of body parts body repairs and parts replacement will be from central repair and warehouse depots not associated with the traditional car dealerships.

5. The classical movie theatre will disappear to be replaced by the improved TV screens in the home and what we might call a 21st century dinner theatre, i.e. plays and shows presented on the screen in restaurant settings with fast food restaurants presenting the shows.

6. Newspapers will be delivered to the home, office or automobile (driver doesn't have to be at the wheel) via FAX machine with customers subscribing only to the parts of the paper they are interested in, e.g. world news, business and markets, local news, police blotters, manufacturing news for construction, automobiles, appliances, mining, fishing, etc. and of course the comics, weather and editorial columns.

7. Cash will have disappeared almost completely by the end of the 21st century replaced by electronic transfers, credit cards and PINs with credit and debit exchanges.

8. Entertainment will see many shifts of location and mode. Baseball, football and basketball will move from the stadium to the TV screen. The games themselves will change to eliminate repetition and boredom with substantial reductions in time. Soccer will become the number one game in the United States replacing football and baseball!

Music will make a radical departure from 20th century volume and content. New musical instruments and electronic controls will reduce volume and increase melody with lyrics to produce an entirely new mode of music for the mass media. The new generations of the 21st century will seize upon these new musical concepts to express their objection and revolt against the "old" generation of the 20th century.

The television soap opera will still be with us, but the theme will change from sexual dysfunction to cultural conflicts expressing the result of the amalgamation of cultures from Asia, Latin America and the Middle East. These conflicts will be highlighted of course by the different sexual mores, the different foods and the different relationships of family values, e.g. religion, gender, education, death, recreation, etc. All of this change to capture the audience's requirement for problem involvement and resolution for their entertainment. As usual, many people without real problems will have to invent them so they can be happy.

Entertainers will continue their efforts in night clubs and television with off the wall and bizarre caricatures trying to out-shock each other, but will have difficulty with the change in audience, namely, preponderance of Hispanics and Orientals in the population.

9. Recreation will expand to a major industry to accommodate the burgeoning population. Everything from bicycling, tennis, skiing, swimming, golf, camping, fishing, hunting, hiking and even bowling will increase with equipment, trainers and guide services. Correspondingly, facilities will have to increase in size and capacity including parks, zoos, golf courses, beaches, bike paths, wilderness areas and touring agents. Note, many recreation activities will take place in the enclosed malls and cities.

10. No change will be more profound than the way our government will function. Notwithstanding the great resistance to change of the political processes and the politicians, the increased pressure of new and expanding technology along with the increased population will demand more representative and accurate government and administrative procedures. Some of the changes anticipated are:

A. Voting will be done out of the home using PINs and the telephones with expanded voting times to as much as one to two weeks. The bedsheet ballot will disappear.

B. The two party political system will have collapsed from its own weight and be replaced by a three or even four party system.

C. The geometry of the states will change to better reflect the composition of the populations living in these areas. Eventual resolution of this problem will result in fewer than the 50 states of the 20th century.

D. The justice system will change to better serve the needs of the public. Hardened criminals will be exported to Asia (Siberia), South America, Africa, etc. in exchange for the hard currency these countries need so desperately. Electronic surveillance systems will replace many police men on the streets and also eliminate much court time, e.g. traffic violation, trespassers, crowd control, etc. Identification of customers or suspects will be greatly simplified and much more accurate with computerized checks on all identification of people and property. Even today where the computers are installed and being used many crimes are being solved by the assimilation and analysis of data. In Los Angeles even old crimes (10 to 15 years old) are being solved with this equipment.

Closed circuit TV will impact just about every aspect of our lives. Improvements in the quality and size of the micro chip will reduce the cost substantially. TV monitoring of factories, stores, warehouses, shopping malls, farm yards, hospital rooms and even private homes and automobiles will be common place. Critical work stations will be constantly monitored, e.g. airline pilots, train operators and ship captains. Video tapes and records will be admissible evidence in the courts. Wire tapping laws will be changed to cope with the great increase in the use of cellular phones, FAX machines, E-mail and computer fraud using telephone lines. With these changes and the ability of television monitors to inspect the interior of private homes via their TV sets, privacy will be severely impacted by technology in the 21st century.

In the courtroom multi-media techniques will use computerized graphics, video taped depositions and of course the retrieval of evidence for jury review and clarification. This will be especially important for the jury to understand complex cases involving technology. Fingerprints and DNA records "On Line" will be instantly available nationwide for checking suspects, employment checks, important financial transactions.

The penal codes of the states and the federal government will be standardized.

Capital punishment will be eliminated with exile and banishment from the country substituting for this form of punishment.

Electronic braces (to replace handcuffs and leg irons) for house arrest will replace jails and prisons reducing the expense of imprisonment. The lap top computer which can be "docked" in the police squad car will become standard so policemen can document crime at the scene and by docking report the crime and receive instant retrieval of all data (fingerprints, police records, etc.) for all suspects and victims.

Biggest problem for the use of all of this technology will be (and is) the training required and acceptance of the new systems and procedures to replace the old way of doing things. Even today most people including professionals don't even know how to type! Institutions must also change to accept this new technology. Many operating departments fear that their functions and jobs will be eliminated with the new technology. However, just as the criminal element takes advantage of the new technology the only way to cope will be with the same technology. Anything less will be victory for the criminal.

E. Illegal aliens will be easier to identify and deported "en mass" from the country.

F. Weapons of mass destruction (nuclear and biological) will be so inexpensive and common that Marshall law with the suspension of all constitutional rights will have to be instituted at all critical locations for public safety, e.g. water supply stations, transportation centers, bridges, tunnels, public conveyances, trains, buses, airplanes, government offices, etc.

G. Taxes will be greatly simplified (as proposed in 1996) and the Congress will seek other methods of regulating social policy. This change will cause substantial economic dislocation by reducing the number of Federal employees (computers will replace) and the number of CPAs who prepare taxes.

11. The ratio of senior citizens to the rest of the populations will increase dramatically causing substantial changes in the socio-economic mix of the country. The distribution of wealth will change with most of the property and wealth being concentrated with the older part of the population. Styles for clothing, automobiles, entertainment and food will be reoriented to capture this wealthy part of the population.

12. The racial mix of the U.S. will be very different in the 21st century. Orientals, mostly Chinese, will make up as much as 30% of the population

which along with Hispanics will make up over 50% of the general population.

13. The legal system in the U.S. will undergo substantial changes because of computers. The improvement in accuracy and quality of legal research will change the way the entire legal process functions. Correspondingly whole new classes of problems will arise as other technological advances materialize. Tort law, civil rights and insurance law will change drastically. Contracts for example will automatically be checked and proofed by word processing computers for all essential contract requirements, i.e. legal subject matter, meeting of the minds, legal consideration, competent parties and mutual assent (offer and acceptance).

The laws, procedures and judgments governing Real Property, Torts, Criminal Law, Civil Rights, Labor, domestic relations and the Commercial Code will be simplified and streamlined with the nationwide use and application of computer records for all disputes. Most importantly dispute process will have immediate access to every judgment and point of law ever made on the particular subject of the dispute. This should enable the parties to resolve the problem before they enter the court room and if they still insist on the hearing, the judge can use the data for his judgment.

Most significantly, the social fabric of the nation enveloped with the new as well as the old technology will embrace these improvements to arrange its life style and values to triumph over the problems of enormous populations, invasions of privacy and threats to health and freedom. As usual though technology comes to us as a double edge sword one side of which will be a cornucopia of benefits and the other side a malignant force that can destroy all of the gains we have made for the last two hundred years. As we have already seen in the later part of the 20th century there are many people and even some countries who not only eschew modern technology (except that which earns money for them), but even try to defeat the use of technology for the benefit of others. We see many older urban centers which should have been abandoned years ago still hanging on by sapping federal funds under the euphemism of "saving our cities". As we know too well from much experience old obsolete and worn out cities must be allowed to pass from the scene to make room for the new urban centers. We see this in nature everyday. The dead branches of the tree or shrub must be shed to make room for the new life at the crown of the tree or the new bloom on the rose bush. Mammals too are also shedding their old dead cells to make room for the new cells, that's how we grow.

Not only will our new urban centers provide our expanding populations with the ideal environment and better life style for the 21st century, but the new centers with their advanced housing, food supplies, education and new style of living will provide the perfect models for extra terrestrial developments on the Moon and Mars.

The new urban centers of the 21st Century will not be without its share of problems. The biggest problem of all will be education for the masses of the population. To realize the benefits of an advanced technological society one must be technologically literate. To be technologically literate one must first be literate and be able to read and speak English. Illiteracy has been a serious handicap in the 20th century since the United States changed from an agricultural to an industrial economy. New and improved technologies of the 21st century with better educational system, and more efficient teaching methods should mitigate if not eliminate this problem completely. Most importantly however, we must remember that the advancement of technology is inexorable. Once the genie is out of the bottle it will not return. If we do not learn how to live with it (and profit by it) it will bury us. Technology has a life force of its own, but with vision and diligence we can control it and pave the way for our future development of the moon and the planets.

CHAPTER 13

LUNAR CITIES
21ST CENTURY URBANIZATION

U rbanization in the 21st Century to accommodate the expanding populations of the world and in particular the United States and Europe will not only reach out into many of the remote areas of the country, but will also begin on other planets in our solar system. Although Mars has been the most tempting of all of the planets because of proximity to the earth (35,000,000 miles), its gravity at the surface of 0.38 of the surface gravity of the earth, its atmosphere and the strong suspicion that there was once life on the planet, the development of lunar stations will undoubtedly have first priority because of the immediate benefits to the earth that can be realized. There are no valid reasons for not doing space explorations and planetary development, and there are many good reasons for such improvements especially installing earth stations on the moon for the enrichment of the quality of life here on earth. Some of the reasons for establishing such stations are:

1. Weather control on the earth. One of the first requirements for controlling the devastating storms on the earth, Hurricanes, tornadoes, floods, monsoons and blizzards, is to establish a thorough and accurate monitoring system. These lunar stations will also monitor forest fires which destroy millions of acres of the county's trees every year. Satellites good as they are just cant monitor the entire planet as well as permanent stations on the moon.

2. Earthquake forecasting with possible control in the future. Only by monitoring the entire planet can accurate measurements be made of the

changes in the horizontal and vertical movements of the tectonic plates on the earth.

3. Control of nuclear weapons and monitoring of nuclear power plants, hospitals and marine vessels.

4. Pollution controls for all soils, waters, and air for the entire planet. Since movements of pollutants in the seas and the atmosphere do not recognize any political boundaries and there is limit to the extent that satellites can monitor these movements, the lunar station is by far the best and most convenient way to control this problem.

5. Astronomical laboratories and space construction facilities for future colonization of Mars and possibly other planets in the solar system.

6. Lunar geological explorations for economical resources that can be mined.

7. Manufacturing facilities for the production of goods and equipment that will be used for lunar colonization and space exploration.

8. Monitoring and control of major earth construction projects, e.g. sea level canal to replace the existing Panama canal, bridge and causeway across the Bering Straights, irrigation of the Sahara desert, etc.

9. Monitor temperature and other ecological changes in the earth's atmosphere and oceans. These observations would also include similar measurements of the polar ice caps and the movement of icebergs in the oceans.

10. Development of agricultural and transportation systems for the lunar populations.

11. The lunar space stations and cities will be the original prototypes for the colonization of the other planets, namely, Mars. Once the lunar stations are operational the adjustments in procedures will be minimal for each of the operations on the other planets.

12. Monitor and maintain inventory control for all agricultural crop and cattle production as well as fish harvest from the seas. This is especially important for those products which are subsidized by the government.

13. A meteor and asteroid monitoring station. Recent revelations by the defense department confirm old suspicions that the earth is constantly bombarded by huge boulders and rocks with huge amounts of energy released in the upper atmosphere (and sometimes on the surface of the earth). The

frequency of these impacts is about one a month setting off a blast equal to a 15-kiloton nuclear explosion. The largest of these explosions occurred on Aug.3, 1963 when a rock 80 feet wide struck south of Africa and produced a blast equal to a one megaton nuclear explosion, or one million tons of high explosives. Fortunately for the earth the October 5, 1997 atmosphere absorbs these hits without much damage to the surface of the planet although in 1908 one such explosion occurred over Siberia when a speeding object exploded in the atmosphere with a force of some 20 hydrogen bombs. and the resulting shock wave flattened hundreds off square miles of forest and reverberated around the world. It is also believed that another such encounter occurred 65 million years ago resulting in the extinction of the dinosaurs. Tracking these meteors and asteroids becomes more and more important as our traffic to and from the moon increases in the 21st century. As of 1997 we have only had six Apollo missions to the moon, but lunar development will require many more and up to this time it appears that the meteors have the right of way so we will have to know where they are and when to expect them. Additional voyages to Mars and the other planets will also require this information.

Construction on the moon will be very different form the basic design and construction practices here on earth. The fact that the ratio of gravity on the moon to the gravity on earth is only 0.166 will dramatically alter the size and make-up of the materials used as well as the conventional methods of load analysis for the various structural members. Everything from the operation of machinery to the distribution of atmospheric gases (essential for sustaining life) will be different than the same or comparable operations here on earth. The basic energy used for all of this lunar development will be nuclear and the first power plants will probably be similar to the power plants used on our submarines here on earth. Solar energy will also play an important role since there are no fossil fuels on the moon. These two sources will make up the total supply of primary energy.

Since there is no atmosphere on the moon and all human or animal habitat must be protected from radiation and extreme temperatures, all urban centers,

residential, agricultural and industrial activity will be "underground".
Transportation between urban centers and other centers of economic activity
will also be underground for the most part although surface transportation is
also practical with proper protection. From a development point of view the
moon presents a most pristine stage for the beginning of human habitation and
the operation of earth oriented commerce and industry. After much home work
here on earth early explorations and reconnaissance will establish the ideal
locations for the various laboratories, staging centers, and urban centers. Many
problems will face the new developers although most of these will be similar to
the problems faced by the early settlers of the new world in the 17th, 18th and
19th century.

Some of the most important task and problems will be:

1. Soil borings, laboratory analysis and measurements of the geological
    formations, radiation and gravity variations will have to be made for all of
    the lunar characteristics for the construction of all of the facilities.
2. Many bridges and tunnels will have to be constructed for the lunar
    transportation system. Along with the transportation tunnels between urban
    centers and other work stations, major port facilities and warehouses will
    have to be constructed for the space vehicles, passengers and freight to and
    from earth.
3. Construction of Electrical Power Transmission Lines, unit sub stations and
    distribution lines from the nuclear power plants to the urban centers, space
    ports and other work stations.
4. Telecommunication and environmental control system for the urban
    centers, earth satellites, space vehicles and lunar transportation rolling
    stock.
5. Water manufacturing plants and storage basins.
6. Agricultural production facilities (farms) for foods that are compatible with
    the lunar environment.
7. Residential accommodations for all personnel. In all probability these
    accommodations will be underground and very likely similar to the living
    quarters on today's nuclear submarines. Tours of duty will be relatively

short because of the limitations of human beings living with reduced gravity. Notwithstanding such limitations recreational facilities and entertainment will be needed to maintain physical and emotional stability for the human personnel. Recreation may include golf, basketball, tennis, etc. although the rules may have to be altered a bit. Entertainment will include music, libraries, television hook-ups with earth satellites, vcr, etc.

8. Lunar transportation systems will include trains, automobiles and trucks, and of course space vehicles for earth flights. All lunar transportation will of course be electrically powered, but note that energy consumption will be relatively small compared to earth because of the substantial reduction of gravity on the moon.

9. A self contained military post to provide security for all lunar operations and to monitor earth operations for violations of international and lunar agreements.

At the risk of oversimplification we may visualize the 21st century urban centers on the moon as totally enclosed "malls" similar to what we see today in 20th century America. As a practical matter the entire center will be underground because of the extreme temperatures and radiation at the surface. The center will therefore have a totally enclosed and controlled environment to allow the occupants to function as normally as possible under the circumstances. The most limiting factor for the use and operation of the center will be the reduced gravity of the lunar surface. Hopefully, new technology will mitigate this handicap, but until then the time of human occupation will be limited to tolerable tours of duty.

The urban centers will contain everything we know of in today's urban centers including shopping malls, restaurants, entertainment centers, recreation facilities, hospitals, offices, light industries, schools, libraries, waste treatment facilities and water supplies, police departments and fire departments and of course residential apartments and housing. There will also be special air treatment centers to recycle the air and any other products of combustion from the enclosed urban centers. None of these important gases can be allowed to escape. They will have to be salvaged for treatment and reuse by the human

occupants. Transportation centers in the urban centers will connect with
transportation tubes to the other lunar work stations, port facilities, power
plants, agricultural farms, food processing plants and laboratories, all located at
other strategic parts of the moon.

How will lunar urbanization take place? Once decisions are made to begin
the work, reconnaissance missions will initiate the first explorations of the lunar
surface. Bivouacs will be established, topographic maps will have to be made,
soil borings drilled, supplies stored, telecommunications established and
schedules developed for the completion of the work and the beginning of the
next missions. On earth, corresponding arrangements will be made including
lunar urban center and work station design, mission quality control programs,
procurement of materials for lunar construction, schedules including
computerized pert programs, personnel recruitment and training, lunar colony
coordination programs, and of course, budget and financial controls.
Although the space program up to this time has been essentially scientific, from
this point forward for the colonization of the moon, the bulk of the development
work will be construction engineering for the building of the urban centers and
their links to the other important lunar stations. In this regard it is significant
that today, 1996, Lunar building contest are being held for the development of
the most efficient remotely controlled equipment that is lightweight and able to
maneuver in the Moon's powdery soil. Once again technology is becoming the
avant guard for the development of new colonies or urbanization of our new
frontiers.

Based on the knowledge and research from the initial missions, the second
phase of the program will include the development of space freighters to haul
the necessary materials to the moon for the Phase II construction program. The
first facilities to be built will be the space ports (two will be required, one for
each side of the moon) and the nuclear power plants with their power
transmission lines to the various unit sub stations. Other projects based on their
priorities will then be in a position to start the construction of their facilities
more efficiently. Since all required power up to this time must be transported
from earth, the completion of this first power plant will be a major step forward
for the lunar development program. Notwithstanding the reduced gravity on the

moon's surface there will still be a great deal of work and energy required to complete the work. Even though a portable power plant will be used in the beginning, a permanent power plant must be made available as soon as possible for the great amount of work to proceed.

The lunar construction program itself will involve the excavation and movement of massive amounts of the lunar crust (mass grading) at the locations of the urban centers, the space ports, transportation tunnels and the important work stations. Foundations will be formed and cast using a new "lunar" cement in lieu of the earth bound portland cement which is based on crushed limestone. Structural framing for the various buildings and other support structures will use magnesium and/or aluminum alloys or possibly plastic members or some combination of these materials.

There will have to be substantial changes in the curricula of present day engineering schools to prepare students to cope with the new technological requirements of the lunar construction and operation of equipment for transportation, power plants, electrical transmission, cycling of waste products, fire protection, communications, etc.. Based on early explorations and testing of the lunar materials, new designs will be required to meet all of the requirements of lunar (and other planetary) development with the most economical use of the native materials and unique environmental conditions.

How much development is possible on the moon? The lunar surface is approximately 14,657,414 square miles or about 22% of the earth's surface, there are no oceans on the moon; in fact there is no water at all, so practically all of the lunar surface can be developed! There may be some limitation on the extent of this development because of the dark side of the moon which is forever hidden from view of the earth, but this lack of vision does not defeat the availability of the development area on the far side. The total lunar surface area is about the same as the size of North America (9 million square miles) plus Europe (3.99 million square miles). One half of the lunar area, say the half which faces the earth all of the time, is about the size of South America (6.879 million square miles). Most importantly, there are no oceans or ice caps on the moon so most all of the surface area is available. However, the lunar surface is not smooth like a sheet of silk. The most conspicuous irregularities of the lunar

surface are the great number of craters some of which are enormous. Without a
doubt these craters are the result of collisions with asteroids and other celestial
debris over the aeons of geologic time since the beginning of the universe.
The other prominent surface features are the "mares" or seas of what appears to
be lava from ancient eruptions or collisions with asteroids. The craters resemble
the volcanic craters on earth and may be of similar origin, but there the analogy
must stop since some of the lunar craters are of such great size. The typical
crater on the moon has a surrounding ring that may rise as high as 20,000 feet
above the lunar surface. The floor of the crater may be higher or lower than the
outside level! Often there may be a mountain peak or peaks in the middle of the
crater. There are also a great number of small craters which extend in rays from
a number of larger craters for hundreds of miles. It is obvious that many
accurate topographic maps will have to be made along with many other test to
determine the best locations for urban centers and the transportation tunnels.

Not only will the materials and all of the engineering criteria for lunar
construction be different from the earth experiences, but with the very unique
topographical differences, a whole new engineering science may be required to
develop the new urban centers and their work stations.

Will our view of the moon from earth be different with the development of
lunar urban centers and work stations? No, the total absence of an atmosphere
with the extreme temperatures between day and night (on the moon) combined
with cosmic radiation will prohibit any human development on the moon's
surface. All development will be under the surface of the moon or in totally
enclosed and shielded structures which should all be invisible to any casual
observer on earth.

What changes on earth can we expect from the development of urban
centers and other work stations on the moon? Historically the most conspicuous
relationship of the moon to the earth is its appearance to viewers on earth and its
effect on the tides of the oceans. Cupid, fishing and deer hunting appear to be
more active with the different phases of the moon, but that's about the extent of
the moon's influence as far as we know. Lunar development however, will raise
many more provocative issues with the nations on earth. Who will decide the
political status of the moon? Who will regulate the mining and other industrial

development? Who will regulate the advertising on the moon? Coca Cola comes to mind! More poignantly perhaps will be the question of lunar surface ownership? Will there be a designated lunar land rush? How will prices and moon titles be established? To answer these questions and many more of course, a new branch of real estate law will have to be developed along with new laws affecting personal property, mining and most importantly, water rights. Needless to say very little has been done to address these questions up to this time, but the issues will confront us very soon and our schools and universities should be investigating the problems today.

INDEX